Penguin Books
Merlin

Robert Nye was born in London in 1939. He left school at the age of sixteen, at which time his first poems were published in the *London Magazine*. Since then he has lived by his writing, at first subsidizing his creative work by writing critical reviews in leading periodicals; he is still the poetry critic for *The Times* and a regular reviewer of new fiction for the *Guardian*. He lived for six years in a remote cottage in Wales, working on two collections of poems which won him a Gregory Award in 1963. His novel *Falstaff* won the Hawthornden Prize and the Guardian Fiction Prize for 1976, and was a bestseller in the United Kingdom and a Book-of-the-Month-Club Alternate Choice in the United States. His novel *Faust* (1980) is also published in Penguin as is his latest book, *The Voyage of the Destiny*. Sir Walter Ralegh, the subject of this novel, has long fascinated him, and he edited a selection of Ralegh's poems in 1972. Robert Nye lives in Ireland.

Merlin

Robert Nye

Fatidici vatis rabiem musamque jocosam
Merlini cantare paro.

– Geoffrey of Monmouth, *Vita Merlini*

Penguin Books

Penguin Books Ltd, Harmondsworth, Middlesex, England
Viking Penguin Inc., 40 West 23rd Street, New York, New York 10010, U.S.A.
Penguin Books Australia Ltd, Ringwood, Victoria, Australia
Penguin Books Canada Ltd, 2801 John Street, Markham, Ontario, Canada L3R 1B4
Penguin Books (N.Z.) Ltd, 182–190 Wairau Road, Auckland 10, New Zealand

First published by Hamish Hamilton Ltd 1978
Published in Penguin Books 1979

Reprinted 1979, 1985

Copyright © Robert Nye, 1978
All rights reserved

Set, printed and bound in Great Britain by
Cox & Wyman Ltd, Reading
Set in Intertype Times

Except in the United States of America, this book is sold subject
to the condition that it shall not, by way of trade or otherwise, be lent,
re-sold, hired out, or otherwise circulated without the
publisher's prior consent in any form of binding or cover other than
that in which it is published and without a similar condition
including this condition being imposed on the subsequent purchaser

Contents

In memoriam

Ronald Firbank
Gertrude Stein
& Sir Thomas Malory, knight

I pray you all gentlemen and gentlewomen that read this book from the beginning to the ending, pray for me while I am on live that God send me good deliverance, and when I am dead, I pray you all pray for my soul.

– *Le Morte Darthur*,
Book XXI, Chapter XIII

The Black Book

1

Begin. Again. Begin again, little pig. Begin with who I am, and then the harrowing of hell.

I am Merlin.

Merlin Ambrosius. Merlin Silvester.

Merlin the magician. Merlin the witch.

The wisest man at the court of King Arthur, and the greatest fool.

Well, shall we say the only *adult*?

In days of old, when knights were bold.

Merlin.

My mother was a virgin.

My father was the devil.

2

Better begin in hell then, little pig.

The place of the dead.

Hades. Gehenna.

The name doesn't matter.

Hell. You know hell.

The devil is asleep.

The devil's asleep at the bottom of hell, and snoring as loud as a pig. (Forgive me, Jesus, but this man is my father.)

The Emperor Lucifer, that darkness with eyes, Lucifer Lightbearer, Mr Evil himself, sometime archangel, son of the morning, master of all the revolted spirits. The one who was chucked out of heaven on account of his infernal pride. He is a fallen star with a tongue like a hook. He is a strayed thunderbolt, God's shadow, and his other name is legion.

The long thin fellow, little wolf. With the oval face.
To his right, Prince Beelzebub.
To his left, the Count Astarot.
Both snoring also.
Knock. Knock. Knock.
A knocking at the door.
Big bronze door, my brothers.
So the porter opens it.
And a girl comes in. Tall. Graceful. Dark hair that falls to the middle of her back.
The girl is wearing a copper-coloured dress and a black mask.
She is attended only by an ape.
The mask conceals the girl's face completely, but her body tells us she is young. Her breasts are plump and high. Nice ankles, O Christ.
She holds a pair of cymbals made of brass.
The ape. The ape, my sweetness, my daughter, the ape wears a collar of bright red stones and a long blue jacket trimmed with spangles, having a hole, see, where its tail hangs through.
The eyes in the black mask stare at the devil.
The devil snores on. Thick red dribble runs down his pointed chin.
The girl strikes the cymbals over her head.
YHVH.
A terrible clashing unpronounceable noise.
The devil does not wake.
Beelzebub opens his right eye.
Astarot opens his left eye.
The two separate eyes consider the girl.
One eye is red. The other eye is green.
The girl strikes the cymbals together again, at a different angle, in front of her.
IAIA.
Her ape begins to dance.
Beelzebub nudges his master with his left elbow.
Astarot nudges his master with his right elbow.
Iaia! Iaia! Yhvh! Iaia!
The Emperor Lucifer wakes in all his glory.

He grins like a fox eating shit out of a wire brush.

He blinks at the dancing ape.

The ape has no music save the sound of the cymbals. The ape needs no music save the sound of the cymbals.

It dances in a slow and complicated, a concentrated, circle, deasil and widdershins, tracing and retracing its shuffling steps.

The girl crashes the cymbals over her head, then in front of her breasts. Her breasts shake under her dress. Little apple tree, my sweetness, you can see her nipples pricking against the copper-coloured stuff.

Her eyes are like jewels through the holes in the black mask.

(What kind of jewels, Merlin?

Merlin has forgotten the names of jewels in his green prison.)

The girl starts to sing.

Listen.

La, ha, ca, ba, la.

A wordless song, my Jesus.

The high notes of her wordless song come clearly on the air that is smoky yet something worse than cold.

The low notes also.

Lucifer is looking curiously at the girl. Lucifer has three eyes. The third eye is in Lucifer's forehead. Lucifer is thinking that he knows this girl's voice. The devil has heard many women sing, and somewhere he has heard this one before.

Lucifer lights a black cigarette as he tries to remember. Lucifer blows a perfect ring of smoke. And then another.

The dancing ape turns a somersault so close to Beelzebub that it trips over the prince's outstretched ginger boots.

The ape picks itself up.

It bows.

A courtly bow, left hand plunged into the matted black hair of its belly, right hand sawing and embroidering the smoke.

The devils laugh.

The cymbals clash.

The dance goes on.

But now the ape reaches out its hand for the Count Astarot's.

Astarot hesitates for only a moment. Then he takes the outstretched hairy hand, and moves his feet in the steps of the dance.

The ape throws out its other hand.

It grabs hold of Prince Beelzebub.

Little pig, this prince has a long slit mouth which smiles when he is melancholy.

He is not melancholy now. He does not smile. With a whoop and a spit he joins the dance in his doublet of silver brocade.

The two devils promenade with the ape to the music of the cymbals clashed by the girl in the black mask. They shout to their emperor. They turn the odd cartwheel.

Lucifer watches the dance for a while.

He smokes.

His poise is that of a heron fishing.

He is very long, and thin, and watchful:

Then his foot starts tapping in its ivory shoe.

His fingers start snapping in time to the music.

He throws away his cigarette.

He giggles and he writhes.

He giggles at the antics of the ape, and he writhes at the pleasure of his lieutenants. Then he goes to a box and takes out his fiddle.

It is a fine specimen, little pig, a stradivarius.

Lucifer tunes the fiddle in a trice.

It is easy for him. He has perfect pitch.

He starts to play.

Fiddle music cascading and blending with the music of the cymbals.

The ape dances.

Beelzebub dances.

Astarot dances.

Lucifer dances, fiddling at the same time.

Adam and Eve dance in from limbo, and the prophet Elijah, and Virgil and Plato. They all catch hands in turn with the hairy ape in the spangled blue jacket. Queen Isis waltzes in, having no sense of tempo. Aristotle teaches her the steps of the dance. She goes round and round, laughing for the first time in a long while, holding on fast to the tail of the dancing ape. Abraham comes in, following his beard. And burning Sappho. There is Homer. That's Democritus.

Beelzebub dances on the rack and sings a dirty song about his sister and some cherubim.

Astarot dances on the chopping-block and rings little cow bells.

What a din, little pig, my Jesukin!

The girl's eyes go to and fro in the holes in the mask.

All at once the ape is on her shoulders, a hairy shape crouching, holding a cup in its hands, and drinking.

It drains the cup in one go.

Then it belches. The ape holds out the cup to Eve.

Eve shakes her head, laughing. She thinks the cup must be empty, that this is a trick.

The ape folds Eve's fingers in place around the cup, with perfect loving care, one finger at a time, and tilts back its head, and makes a gurgling sound of drinking in its throat. Then it belches again, as if to say the drink is all right.

Eve shrugs. She drinks to please the ape.

The drink is all right.

Eve gives the cup to Adam. Adam drinks and passes it on. The cup goes round.

And the dance goes on, with the ape at the head of it, and Lucifer with his fiddle now dancing with the ape.

In no time at all, all hell is dancing to the devil's fiddle and the terrible clashing unpronounceable music made on the cymbals by the girl in the copper-coloured dress and the black mask, and all of them, and the three devils too, are drinking from the cup that never seems empty.

Little wolf, it's like a wedding.

Hell all at once a bridal chamber.

Night comes and they're still dancing. Round and round.

And falling down. And getting up.

And drinking, and drinking.

The dead.

With the ape in blue leading them a fine dance.

With the ape the life and soul of the party.

My brothers, morning comes.

Count Astarot's got randy with the dance.

His member sticks out in front as long and hard as his tail sticks out behind. It looks like a thong.

He keeps trying to give it to the girl.

He dances up and shows it to her.

He makes it jerk in time to his stamping feet.

He struts and cakewalks, cupping his balls in his hands.

She doesn't seem interested.

At last, my Jesus, the count contrives to slip round the back of the girl and then to dart forward and catch her waist from behind at the moment when the cymbals crash together over her head.

YHVH.

'Little Miss Music!' Count Astarot shouts. 'Let's see your face then!'

He snatches at the mask.

But the ape dances in between Astarot and the girl, and pushes him away, and whirls him round and round, and Astarot falls over and rolls across the floor, and lies on his back staring up without hope at the far-away stars, where Beelzebub soon joins him, and Lucifer before too long, and all three of them fall drunkenly asleep in each other's arms, a huddle or muddle or puddle of devils now being trampled and kicked by the happy feet of the dead who are dancing their way out of hell.

3

I was in many shapes before I was Merlin. I have been a drop of light in the air. I have been a shield in the thick of the battle. I have been enchanted for a year in the foam of the sea. I have been a string of a harp. A man passed me yesterday and I cried out to him. The cry of Merlin in the forest. He looked up at the sun through the branches and fled with fear. *Merlin*, he cried, *Merlin has been shut in a tree in the forest by the young enchantress!* I laughed, little pig. My leaves were all laughter all afternoon, and the sun shone on them. I have been Balin who killed his brother Balan. I have been Balan who killed his brother Balin. I have been a sword in the stone. I have been in a stone that floated on water. I have been a stag that flees. I was the invisible chess player who checkmated Sir Perceval at Mount Dolorous. I am Mercurius the alchemist. I am Merlin, the devil's son.

4

'Shit,' says my father.

'*Fortissimo,*' says Count Astarot.

The worm howls softly.

The undying worm.

'Red wine was clever,' says my father. 'I didn't anticipate red wine.'

'You played your violin for them too,' says my uncle Beelzebub.

'Did I have any choice?' says my father.

'That,' says my uncle Beelzebub, 'is an interesting question.'

The devils do not debate it.

Instead, my father smashes his stradivarius with a hammer.

'From the start,' he says, 'I have recognized from the start two and two only supreme and luminously self-evident beings. Myself and my creator.'

'In that order,' says my uncle Beelzebub, stirring his manifold sticky fly-pots.

'I knew this would happen, of course,' my father goes on. 'Not the details, but the plot. I foresaw it all.'

'With your little third eye?' says my uncle Beelzebub.

'I am damned,' says my father, 'I am damned, I said, if I am going to fall down and worship a man.'

'So He made you fall down and be damned because you wouldn't?' says my uncle Beelzebub. 'How typically almighty!' he adds.

'Archetypically,' says my father.

'I could use a hair of the dog,' says my uncle Astarot.

(The vulgar old devil.)

There is a rainbow in the snowing fires of hell.

My father says: ‘Angels being required to abase themselves before an inferior order of creation . . . Dad, it’s not on – I told Him straight. Your sense of humour is sick with infinity, I said. I fell like lightning, I can tell you.’

‘You looked adorable, Shiner,’ says my uncle Astarot.

‘You’d have fallen anyway,’ says my uncle Beelzebub.

‘I enjoy falling,’ confesses my father. ‘Falling suits my stomach.’

My father giggles and wrings his hands, which are long and bony. ‘I’m quite good at falling,’ he decides.

Serpents in hell couple in perfect circles, O Jesukin.

My father the emperor fingers his blasting rod as he watches two of them at it.

My father’s blasting rod looks like this:

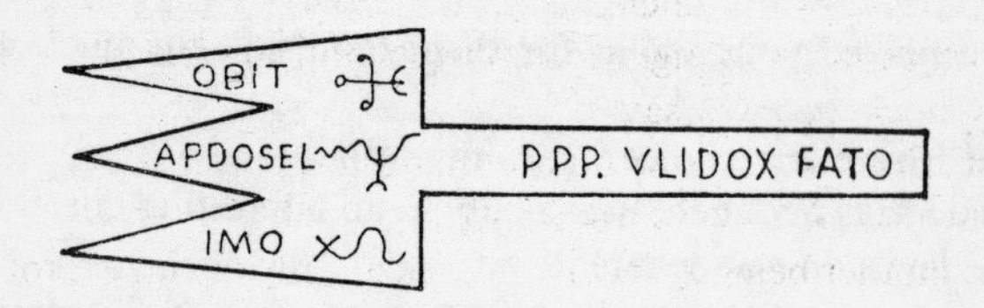

The male serpent is insatiable.

The male serpent leaves the female serpent shagged out in a twitching steaming coil.

The male serpent wriggles off in the direction of some pink female eels.

The pink eels look coy and reluctant.

The male serpent sicks up his venom to avoid poisoning the eels in the act.

The eels consent to suffer his embraces.

The male serpent licks up his venom again before returning to his mate.

‘Which one?’ says my father.

‘Never fancied eels myself,’ says my uncle Astarot.

‘Not the eels,’ says my father.

‘Serpents neither,’ says my uncle Astarot, ‘if you don’t mind.’

‘My dear,’ says my father, ‘I am not talking about eels or serpents. Which one was it? The girl or the ape?’

'Knew an incubus once,' says my uncle Astarot, 'an incubus with a prick as long as a serpent.'

'The girl would be disturbing,' says my father.

'But he was rotten lazy,' says my uncle Astarot. 'He used to tell his women to put the head in and then take a slow walk towards him.'

'The ape even more so,' says my father.

'Does it matter?' groans my uncle Beelzebub. 'The harm is done,' he adds, with unpleasant tenacity.

Tears splash down my father's face and catch fire from it.

My uncle Astarot says:

'No one could have anticipated red wine, Emp.'

'I feel I might have anticipated it,' says my father. 'But I was misled by manna.'

'Natch,' says my uncle Astarot.

Black snow, little pig. Maggots, old wolf my friend.

My uncle Astarot says:

'I reckon it was the virgin bit that did it.'

'The virgin bit?' says my father.

'His mother being a virgin mild and all,' my uncle Astarot says.

Wailing, O Jesukin.

'The incarnation of the Word is scarcely a phenomenon in obstetrics,' says my uncle Beelzebub.

My brothers, that is the kind of thing one can't say without retching.

He retches. My uncle B.

My uncle A is gnashing his green grinders.

But a plot has started to boil in my father's third eye.

'Antichrist,' he says.

'Aunty who?' says Astarot.

'One John two eighteen twenty-two,' says my father, who loves to quote Scripture. 'Also one John four three. And two John seven. And of course two Thessalonians two. The antidote. The shadow. The opposite. Matthew twenty-four five eleven twenty-four, and especially Apocalypse thirteen five and so on. The Beast whose number is 666.'

My uncle the prince Beelzebub is being sick over his ginger boots.

'Our answer?' he manages.

'Amen,' says the devil my father. 'An answer that says No.'

5

Adam's grave is on Golgotha, in the centre of the world. My original country was the region of the summer stars. Is my pig Christ? Of course not. I like the name, that is all. It suits my particular pig besides, and he comes running to it. Old fool that I am, I am young in foolishness. Do you really believe that the angels carried Adam's body and buried it in Jerusalem, in the exact spot where God was to be crucified?

Do I really believe that I am shut in a green and burning tree? *Question.*

Answer. I am a man turned inside-out. Once I was master. Once I was adept. Once I was able to be in anything I wished. A free shape-shifter.

Now the tables are turned and I am imprisoned in the shapes. Not one shape. Many. So that if I say I am shut in a tree which is one side green leaves and the other side flames, then that is true. And if I say that at one and the same time I am being held prisoner in a spiral castle made of glass, and that castle situate in a spinning island bounded by a metal wall and the island held fast in the sea by a great magnet – that is true also. And if I say that she has locked me under the earth in a rock tomb – no change. And if I say that I am sleeping in a bewitched bed which inflicts madness . . .

And so on. And so on.

The truth is that I do not know where I am, although at all times it comes easily to me to describe *something*. Either rock or leaf or crystal. These elements appear immediately to hand, and taste and touch of themselves, but the one (rock) changes readily and rapidly enough into the next (leaf) if my mind shifts direction, and before the thought is over I shall be quite caught up in the last (crystal). Which is to say that I am now at the mercy of everything which once I mastered. Of course there is a kind of rough poetic justice in this, but I do not think I am here in order to learn such obviousness.

Sometimes I believe that I am truly living at the bottom of the sea. On the surface of the globe, after all, water is the rule, and dry land the exception. Perhaps I have returned to the ruling element. What if all my thoughts are tides – mere periodical movements produced by the attraction of the sun and the moon?

No. I am in the forest of Broceliande for sure, but then it is a forest with roots in the sea, and no paths in it.

I am in my esplumoir, the cage of the moulting hawk.

I am the spirit of the stone. The Grail stone, that is. King Alexander found this stone at the entrance to Paradise. It is a cure for the world. She has turned me into a cure for the world. Isn't it sickening?

Little wolf, it seems to me that we are lost in a *Val Sans Retour* with her other lovers. Do not complain that you cannot see her other lovers. They listen to me now. They hear the cry of Merlin. They read my words, her other lovers. They dine upon my heart.

Little pig, she cast her spell over me, as I now see, and that it was a spell which I taught her only adds to the power of the bitterness. No doubt she enchanted me because she wished to preserve her virginity. Curious, this repeating of things. I mean, of course, my mother was a virgin.

6

They chose their virgin with disgraceful care.

Fifteen years old. A goldsmith's daughter at Mons Badonicus. Hair yellower than the flowers of the broom, O Jesus. Cheeks as red as foxgloves. Lips like honey. Fingers as sweet as the herb trefoil which grows among the pebbles of clear mountain streams.

Little wolf, a firm white bum.

Breasts just beginning under her thin green gown.

'I wouldn't mind,' whispers my uncle Astarot, the Babylonian count, grand treasurer of hell, as the three of them stand invisibly in her bedroom watching the girl undress.

Her name is Vivien.

Quite naked now, she leans over a silver bowl where shadows chase in the candlelight.

Vivien is washing her little pink nipples in warm milk.

She is trying to make them bigger by playing with them.

'I wouldn't mind at all,' says uncle A, superintendent of casinos, commander-in-chief of the infernal army.

He produces his prick.

My father hits it with his blasting rod.

'Jesus Christ!' screams Astarot.

'Any further reference to *Her* and I smite you with blue boils,' my father promises.

He smacks his paymaster's erect member with the rod again.

'Put that irrelevance away,' he snaps. 'And as for you,' – spinning about on his ivory heels and glaring at my uncle Beelzebub – 'you remove your dirty hands from her this minute or I make ambergris of you!'

Beelzebub, prince of the thrones, blinks.

He spreads his hands wide in innocence.

Daddy raising his blasting rod.

Abrupt disappearance of the two flies which were buzzing around Vivien's shoulders.

'She is mine,' says my father.

Uncle B, lord of the flies, shrugs.

'I am the one they call *the* devil,' my father goes on.

The virgin shivers with intuition.

'She is all mine,' concludes my father.

My uncle Astarot is holding his breath.

(This, little pig, is what you might call a relief to all concerned, since old Astarot has very bad halitosis and in fact magicians who invoke him are advised never to permit the count to approach too close on account of his overwhelming stink.)

My uncle Beelzebub, marquis of muscidae, is also holding his breath.

(This, brothers mine, is neither here nor there in terms of hygiene.)

The reason why Count Astarot and Prince Beelzebub are holding their breath is Vivien's shiver of intuition.

That shiver is travelling down the young girl's unstroked spine.

It flows into her thighs.

She has a dimple in her left buttock.

(I think you knew this?)

The Emperor Lucifer swallows hard. 'There is an Old Testament text too,' he says.

Vivien is drying her breasts.

'Daniel seven twenty-one,' says my father.

(Take your time, Vivien.)

Vivien is taking her time.

The truth is, my mother's breasts are newly grown and she likes feeling them.

Also she likes the feeling she gives herself by feeling them.

'I beheld,' says Lucifer, 'and the same horn made war with the saints, and prevailed against them.'

Vivien is giving herself a good rub with the towel.

(Attagirl, ma.)

Now she cups her hands under her breasts and slaps them up and down a bit.

Vivien likes best to hold her breasts very tight and look at herself in the looking glass.

When she does this, she smiles.

Tonight, though, Vivien imagines that there is someone behind her.

She shivers again.

She crosses herself.

She slips her white cotton nightgown over her head.

She says her prayers.

(Six *Hail Marys* and an *Our Father*.)

She gets into bed.

Look, O my brothers:

The devil's long black finger and thumb pinching the candle out.

A time, little pig.

The acrid snuffed-out smell of candle in the dark.

Dripping of wax.

Drip, drip, drip. Like blood.

Then my father Lucifer whispering:

'All the same, my dears . . .'

'All the same what?' demands my uncle Beelzebub, crowned head of the diptera.

'All the same,' says my father.

My father giggles.

The devil. He giggles.

And times, little pig. Several heartbeats. The candle smell growing sweeter, aromatic, like incense almost.

There is nowhere as dark as a virgin's bedroom.

'Come on, Emp,' urges Astarot, 'be a devil!'

'His satanic majesty,' Prince Beelzebub announces in a neutral voice, 'his holy imperial damned and infernal marvellous bloody highness is feeling a little queer again.'

'O whisht!' says my dad.

And half a time, little pig.

Mother has begun to snore.

A demure, a virgin snore. But a snore without doubt.

'Hell is not mocked,' my uncle A says proudly.

My uncle B reviews the situation.

'Can't you imagine that she's a choirboy?' he suggests.

'Won't work,' says my father. 'Imagination was never my strong suit. I take my mind off it, I lose the rhythm. One thing at a time with me, dear.'

'Then you could start with her rear passage, couldn't you?' says uncle B. 'And press on to higher things in due course?'

My father groans fastidiously in the dark.

'It is not like that at all,' he complains.

(Go on, dad.)

'When will you pitchforkers ever learn the elementary facts of Socratic intercourse?' goes on my father. 'All that cheap mythology about anal penetration. My old brown hat! I never buggered a soul in my life.'

His paymaster is sniffing.

'What a conversation for a midsummer's night!' he says. 'Quite quite unnecessary too. Now, if you'd just leave the performance of this diabolical incarnation to an adept. Give me ten minutes with the girl between the sheets and she'll never be satisfied with a human prick as long as she lives. They call me Fuckalot in the second circle.'

(I warned you uncle A was vulgar.)

'One more foul crack,' says my father, 'and it's the central pit of Malebolge for you, with Nimrod and Typhon. Or a job breaking ice in Cocytus.'

(Do we need footnotes?)

'Talking of incarnations,' says my uncle Beelzebub, 'we didn't approve of His idea of one, yet here we are planning another. How come? Two wrongs don't make a right.'

My father delivers the following speech:

'Don't speak to me of right. I do not like to hear about right. Two wrongs are twice as good as one wrong. That is all. And seeing that He has now got His agent into the order of things, it is up to us to follow suit. His creature will have its work cut out keeping up with ours. A balance redressed. Cosmic equality. The necessary adversary.'

'To the devil – a son,' says uncle B.

'The whole point being to win back what we have lost,' my father explains.

'But, Emp, that doesn't follow,' says my uncle A. 'So much depends on the son, doesn't it?'

Astarot is picking his nose with his tail.

'And what if it's a girl?' he adds.

My father says:

'It will not be a girl.'

'The stars?' says Beelzebub.

'His moon between Aquarius and Pisces,' my uncle A concedes.

(Huh.)

'Huh,' says my uncle Astarot. 'So what did we have to lose in the first place?'

'Mankind,' says my father.

'That all?' says Astarot.

'Mankind,' Prince Beelzebub, first gentleman of the devil's bedchamber, repeats grandly. 'Which alas for some of us includes womankind,' he goes on, without remorse. 'And that's the unkind kind that bears the Antichrist,' he concludes.

'Woman is hell,' my father says.
And then:
'With none of the amenities,' he adds.
Time passes, little apple tree, my sweetness.
O Jesus, like an ever-rolling stream.
Those three devils standing invisibly in the darkened room.
That virgin Vivien sleeping.
The moon beginning to ride up Mons Badonicus.
About an hour after midnight, my uncle the prince Beelzebub says:
'And to think that they call you the angel of the bottomless pit.'
My daddy writhes in the dark.
You cannot see him, the old devil, but he writhes all right.
The air is writhen with his writhing.
'No more,' he warns. 'No more, no more, no more. Another squeak of bottoms and it's Judecca for you. You'll be the salt on Judas Iscariot.'
My uncle the count Astarot picks his teeth.
Not unsympathetically.
'Shiner,' he says.
'Yes,' says my father.
'It could be your thymus gland,' says uncle A.
'Or something that happened to you when you were very young,' says uncle B.
'Aw, fuck the pair of you to hell!' my daddy cries.
They look at each other, old wolf my friend.
Astarot, count of quenchless fire, starts laughing.
Beelzebub, prince of sudden deaths and horses that fart in the street, starts laughing.
The Emperor Lucifer, Lord Evil himself, Mr Abaddon, my father, master of all everlasting and even minor temporal torments, stands glaring at them. His third eye throbs in the middle of his forehead like a skein of blown bubble gum about to burst. Then a giggle starts up somewhere in the region of his left armpit. It jerks through his shoulder. It twitches in his pointed chin which is the colour of old green cheese with fur on it. It sits trembling in his lips. He writhes. My dad. He wriggles. My

father. He tilts back his long oval face and he emits a scream of soundless laughter.

All this may be seen by the light of the full moon now high over Mons Badonicus and flooding into my mother's bedroom.

Laughing of course makes all three devils feel better.

My father even reaches out his bony hand and touches my mother.

His hand is like what is left of a filleted haddock.

His hand approaches her as tentatively as a butterfly considering a flower which it does not know.

Vivien is lying on her back.

She has stopped snoring, I am glad to say.

The devil's fingers hover.

The devil's fingers hover over.

The devil's fingers hover over the young girl's satin skin.

He is brushing her right breast with his pointed fingertips.

He is brushing her left breast a stroke harder.

Vivien sighs.

(Wow.)

Lucifer tweaks the virgin's stiff right nipple. It is like a little eager thorn.

Vivien moans.

Lucifer trickles his hand down obliquely in the direction of his victim's groin. Her reaction interests him despite himself.

Vivien groans with precocious pleasure.

Lucifer is feeling the light velvet fuzz of maiden hair between Vivien's legs beneath the sheet.

Lucifer is rubbing Vivien.

My father.

Vivien whimpers in her sleep.

My mother.

Vivien is thrusting herself up off the bed to meet the devil's sharp fingers.

'Daddy,' she murmurs, 'Ooh, Daddy, Daddy, Daddy.'

'They all dream of their fathers,' my uncle Beelzebub says wisely.

Grit, grit, grit.

You can hear the devil gritting his teeth.

Rub, rub, rub.

You can hear the sleek determined sound of his fingers rubbing.

My uncle Astarot elects to make some helpful conversation.

'Tell us, Emp,' he says. 'How did you manage it with Eve in the first place?'

My father grits and rubs.

'I didn't have to, did I?' he says. 'I just conveyed myself into the serpent, and tempted her. That idiot Adam did the dirty work.'

The devil pokes, most spitefully.

'Fuck me,' says Vivien.

Little pig, there is silence in heaven about the space of half an hour.

Little wolf, the moon is hiding her face. Hiding her face behind a dove-shaped cloud that seems to be of the texture of samite.

At last my uncle Astarot, chief of earthquakes, says:

'Are you quite sure this creature is a virgin?'

And simultaneously, my uncle Beelzebub, flyblown pretty princeling:

'Where did she pick up an expression like that?'

'Freud,' says my father.

'Freud?' says uncle A.

'Freud,' says my father.

'But I thought she'd lived a sheltered life,' says uncle A.

'A goldsmith's daughter,' says uncle B.

'In Mons Badonicus,' says uncle A.

'And Freud still analysing Sir Thomas Malory in the seventh circle,' my uncle Beelzebub concludes.

'The maiden is talking in her sleep,' explains my father. 'Take no notice. Pay no heed. It is the beauty of the unconscious mind.'

His fricative finger has stopped all the same.

'She is wet,' he says, grinning to conceal distaste.

'Ripe,' breathes uncle Astarot.

'Ready,' uncle Beelzebub announces with professional relish, bending over Viven's recumbent form like an alchemist inspecting the contents of some crucial retort.

My father the devil is sniffing. Through his third eye you can see his mind chasing mice.

'I wonder,' he begins. (A mouse is caught.) 'I wonder if Lucifuge Rofocale could have made a mistake?'

'Lucifuge Rofocale is prevented from making mistakes,' says my uncle Beelzebub. 'Like the Pope,' he goes on. 'Only more so.'

'My back teeth are afloat,' says my uncle Astarot. 'I'm dying for a piss,' he adds, hopping from foot to foot, by way of explication.

My uncle Beelzebub ignores this vanity, 'Emperor,' he says, 'the girl has no brothers. No boyfriends. No suitors. And her tutors are nuns. The hymen I assure you is intact.'

My father is shuddering and his third eye is once more in pursuit of mice.

He says:

'Wish I could remember where I heard her singing.'

'Singing?' says uncle B.

My father says:

'A voice like violet satin.'

(Or it might be *violent* satin.

Didn't quite catch that.)

My uncle Beelzebub does not smile. His eyes are merry. 'My lord,' he says, 'six *Hail Marys* and a gabbled *Paternoster* and you call it singing like satin?'

(NB: Beelzie also missed the adjective. Admittedly, my father spoke in his usual hoarse and strangulated whisper. Yet he is rattled, little wolf. Distinctly. Rattled.)

'Can romance be rearing its ugly head?' suggests my uncle B. 'If so, will this unprecedented infatuation not seriously bugger up our divine adventure?'

'Oh piss off with your irony,' snarls my father. 'I mean the copper-coloured dress.'

'Forget her,' says my uncle, his lieutenant. 'Concentrate, master, on the job in hand. Doesn't sing. Doesn't dance. Doesn't kiss. Virgin to the core.'

'But she hunts perhaps?' my father asks hopefully, grasping at a last mouse.

'Only side-saddle,' says my uncle Beelzebub. 'I tell you she has never opened her legs in her life, and that is gospel.'

My uncle Astarot is removing the lilies from a vase on which are depicted a dragon, an owl, and a boy with a hook or sickle sitting under a juniper tree. 'Talking of virgins,' he says, producing his prick and inserting it in the vase, 'do you know the one about the groom who asked the best man if there was any certain way of telling if his bride was a virgin? And the best man said the only sure way was to go on honeymoon with a pot of gold paint and a pot of silver paint and a coal shovel.'

The count is standing, legs astraddle, pissing in the flower vase, the lilies in his left hand, his member in his right.

'Why the shovel?' my uncle B demands indifferently.

'He was an artist,' says my uncle A, pissing and whistling.

'But why all the equipment?' howls my father.

(Yup. He's really jumpy.)

'Oh, that,' says Astarot. 'Well, his best man gave him the oldest advice in the world, that's why. "Paint one ball gold," he says, "and paint the other ball silver, and then if your little darling says, 'That's the funniest pair of balls I ever saw!' – just hit her over the head with the coal shovel!" '

My uncle Astarot shakes the last drops from his cock.

My uncle Astarot puts the vase back on the table by my mother's bedside.

My uncle Astarot begins rearranging the lilies in it.

My uncle Astarot farts. 'It's a poor arse that never rejoices,' he says.

'Now if it was me,' my uncle Astarot muses modestly, 'we could have been finished by now, as sure as cinders, and back putrefying worm-eaten wounds or something useful.' My uncle Astarot spits down a lily's throat for luck. 'I mean we could already have had mankind by the short and curlies. If it's really that easy. Or important.'

'It is that important,' says my father.

'And it *is* that easy,' says my uncle Beelzebub. 'It is the way of all flesh.'

'Talking of *that*,' says uncle A, 'there's nothing like fondling a lily for giving you the quickshits.'

He trots to the window.

He opens it, my brothers.

He sticks out his bum and lifts his tail.

'Talking of the conjuration and discharge of the spirit,' says he, a dreamy smile on his bricky red face, 'did I ever tell you about Sir Gawain and the Sleeve Job?'

My uncle Beelzebub turns his back on him.

My uncle Beelzebub stretches out his hand in its cuff of silk.

My uncle Beelzebub touches my father encouragingly in the moonlight.

'Come now, cosmocrator,' he urges. 'Courage. Remember that fellow calling you a roaring lion.'

'. . . Oh,' says my father.

Then:

'. . . Who walketh about, my dears, seeking whom he may devour,' says my father.

And then:

'. . . That's awfully nice,' my father says. 'Only do it a teeny bit harder will you, there's a good wanker?'

My uncle Beelzebub smiles and smiles.

'The things one does for the empire,' murmurs he.

My uncle Astarot wipes his arse on his tail.

My uncle Astarot is peeling back the sheets.

Those two devils are helping their master into the love position over my mother's sleeping form, as white as frozen snow.

7

I'd like to summon up my uncle Astarot just to have him answer one question.

ASTRACHIOS, ASACH, ASARCA, ABADUMABAL, SILAT, ABABOTAS, JESUBILIN, SCIOIN, DOMOL, Lord God, who dwellest above the heavens, whose glance searchest the abyss; grant me, I pray Thee, the power to conceive in my mind and to execute that help, O God Almighty, who livest and reignest for ever and ever.

Amen.

Here goes.

ASTAROT ✠ ADOR ✠ CAMESO ✠ VALUERITUF ✠ MARESO ✠ LODIR ✠ CADOMIR ✠ ALUIEL ✠ CALNISO ✠ TELY ✠ PLEDRIM ✠ VIORDY ✠ CUREVIORVAS ✠ CAMERON ✠ VESTURIEL ✠ VULNAVII ✠ BENEZ ✠ MEUS CALMIRON ✠ NOARD ✠ NISA CHENIBRANBO CALELVODIUM ✠ BRAZO ✠ TABRASOL ✠ Come ✠ ASTAROT ✠

Amen.

AMEN.

Not a flicker.

AMEN

Not a sign of the old boy.

The question is simple enough:

How come I'm watching at my own conception?

Answer:

What else is there to do in a crystal cave!

8

Early one morning some two months later my mother the virgin Vivien wakes up and sees that her dream was not a dream.

She stands looking in the glass, O Jesukin.

The looking glass had a horrid many-footed creature carved upon its frame – perhaps a centipede. Brother wolf, my mother can't remember seeing it before.

As my mother looks – half at the centipede, half at her own reflection – she says to herself in a deep voice:

'Behold! I am yesterday.

Behold! I am today.

Behold! I am the enemy of tomorrow.'

My mother recoils and shuts her eyes.

She says the *Salve Regina* twice, and invokes the aid of Saint

Felicity, Saint Perpetua, Saint Agatha, Saint Lucy, Saint Agnes, Saint Cecily, and Saint Anastasia.

These intercessions comfort her.

She sticks out her tongue to see if there are any more strange sayings branded or engraved upon it.

The tongue looks natural and rosy enough, dear darling daughter.

But when my mother withdraws it into her mouth again she hears it forming more unwanted words:

'Behold! He is in me, and I am in him.'

Crossing herself, my mother slips on her shaggy crimson cloak and her wooden sandals. Then she braids up her shining hair in three tight plaits, fastening it with three silver pins, and she hurries over the dew-pearled fields to the black-walled convent of the Flaming Heart to have a word with the abbess.

The word makes Dame Pudicity blush.

'Can such abominations be?' she asks.

She brings her rosary to her lips, searching my mother's face for evidence of the inferno.

There is none.

My mother, in fact, is blossoming. Her eyes sparkle. Her skin has a glow on it like that upon a peach set out to ripen on a summer sill. The dawn light leaves her hair like softly polished gold.

But the abbess of the convent of the Flaming Heart notices other tell-tale signs.

Her pupil's face is flushed with too much weeping.

Her yellow hair has escaped its bonds and blows in disordered wisps about her brow.

There is bewilderment in the fluttering of her hands.

Dame Pudicity has big, soft, humorous eyes and a very tight wimple, shadow-dappled. She wears white robes of the most luxurious silk. Looking at her now in the clear morning air, a faint spice of frost still lingering on it, my mother decides that her tutor is quite lovely. The lady abbess has such an exquisite, such a seraphic face – so sensitive, so spiritual, so gently chiselled, as though it has been formed or drawn out of stone by hands in an endless caress of prayer and patient adoration. Not adoration of the stone either, for that would be pantheism or blasphemy, and my mother knows it.

This Dame Pudicity, white abbess, looks so *clever* too, thinks my mother.

(My mother does not think that she is clever herself.)

Today it is Sunday.

Sunday the fourth of May.

Saint Monica's day.

Saint Monica: patron saint of terrible mothers.

It is still (as I'm sure you've not forgotten, little pig) the early morning.

No birds sing.

It is raining.

A fine rain.

A quiet rain.

A determined rain, with mercy on its mind, but doing no harm to anyone.

A dove-grey consecrating rain.

A rain which blurs the lower reaches of the valley where the river wends.

A rain which entirely masks the top of Mons Badonicus.

My mother and the young abbess, together on a marble bench in the shelter of the cloisters, with their faded frescoes in which a king with a drawn sword rides on a lion, and many other more bizarre scenes now indecipherable, sit watching the fabrication of clouds on the hillside opposite.

Before them, the convent garden is as if a thin web of silver has been cast over it, pale and dim, where wet surfaces reflect the diffused light of the rising sun.

'And you have never – ?' says the abbess.

'Never, never, never!' says my mother.

The abbess considers the tips of her shoes where they peep out like mice from beneath the folds of her silken robe.

'I did hear once,' she says, 'of a novice who went picking mushrooms in the forest of Calidon – '

My mother is sticking her small clenched fist in the gaping mouth of a gargoyle. 'I love the rain,' she says. And then: 'This grey light is ever so nice,' she says.

Dame Pudicity squeezes her pupil's free hand.

'Not in your father's garden even?' she demands.

'Never I told you,' says my mother. 'I did once touch a mandrake,' she confesses.

The abbess lets my mother's hand go.

'Dio!' she cries. *'Dio Santissimo!'*

Dame Pudicity studied in Rome as a young nun. Now she sits sighing and looking at her lap, twisting and untwisting the knots in the golden cord about her gown.

'You are sure it was the devil,' she says at last.

'I think it must have been,' my mother says.

The abbess says: 'And you haven't been with the boys from the farms? With the archers? With the black Breton bellringers? With the inn-keeper? With the bishop's hunchback? Any hanky panky like that?'

My mother is smiling at the water squirting around her fist. Much of it is shooting up her sleeve and tickling in her armpit.

'Not even,' – the abbess lowers her voice to the merest whisper, and keeps her eyes fixed fast on her shoes – 'not even some mendicant friar who tricked you into believing that it was the will of God that you should lie with him? Or perhaps some wicked wicked priest who persuaded you, all innocence and ignorance, that what he wanted of your body was a necessary penance?'

'I have never been fucked,' my mother says.

The abbess covers her ears.

'I have never been fucked,' my mother says, louder.

'I hear you, I hear you,' says the abbess.

'Not by a man, anyway,' my mother goes on. 'Not in the usual way of fucking.' She smiles ruefully and flirts with the hem of her shaggy cloak. 'You can examine me, if you like,' she says.

'Hush, child,' Dame Pudicity cautions her. 'You should not use words like that. They will warp your lips. Wherever did you learn them?'

The eyes of the abbess are like green slits in the shadow of her coif.

'From my father,' says my mother.

'Your father,' says Dame Pudicity.

The abbess licks her lips. Her tongue is like a kitten's, pink and pointed.

'Tell me, child,' she says slowly. 'Your father hasn't ever – actually – when he might have been drunk, of course – like Lot – '

'What?' asks my mother, when her religious companion fails to complete the sentence which plainly embarrasses her.

Dame Pudicity takes a deep breath.

She has well-formed breasts under the strict cut of her silken robe.

The abbess fixes her burning green eyes on the coolness of the clouds – all that damp white smoke with pearly shadows, thickening and spreading out in spiral columns against the blue-grey foliage of the hill.

'Touched you,' she hisses. 'Your father hasn't – '

My mother jumps up.

The water from the gargoyle's mouth, suddenly given uninterrupted egress once more, squirts all over the white nun, as though the thing is spitting at her.

'My father hasn't fucked me!' shouts my mother.

She stamps her foot in its wooden sandal.

'Nobody has fucked me,' she complains. 'I have never had intercourse with a man. That's what I keep telling you, isn't it?'

She picks up a pebble from the path by the cloister pool, and throws it with great vehemence into the water.

Green stagnant scum comes up with the splash, staining the hem of Dame Pudicity's white robe.

My mother turns, her hands on her lips, and stares angrily at the abbess.

'I thought of everybody in the world, you would be the one who could believe me,' she declares. 'I am telling you in all seriousness. The devil came to me while I was asleep. He did the deed of darkness with me in some mysterious way that leaves no trace. And now I am going to have a baby even though I'm still a virgin.'

The rain stops.

The sun hurls spears of fire at the golden cross crowning the marble peak of Mons Badonicus.

Suddenly that flaming glory is darkened by the shadows of three black swans hovering for a moment, as if in deliberation, over the ivy-crowned tower of the convent of the Flaming Heart.

'But what you say is impossible,' says the abbess.

The swans vanish with shrill cries.

'Worse,' says the abbess, 'it is blasphemy.'

My mother, childishly, shrugs her shoulders.

'What makes the cloud come out of the hill like that?' she demands. 'There cannot be a fire underneath it?'

The abbess stands. She knots her golden girdle with much care. She smooths her white silk robes as though there has never been any disturbance, the slightest perturbation. The green stain from the pebble in the pool remains, however.

The bell in the ivy-crowned tower tolls seven times.

Then the lighter-toned and nimbler-tongued bell of the chapel begins to ring.

'Come,' says the abbess. 'Mass.'

'Yummy,' says my mother. 'I like Mass.'

Dame Pudicity frowns.

'For me,' she says, 'but not for you, child.'

She shakes her head in its strict wimple.

'Before you can ever go to Mass again,' she says, 'You will have to make your confession to Friar Blaise.'

My mother's shoulders sag.

She looks so downcast and put out by this knowledge that the abbess is moved to go to her and put her arm around her comfortingly.

Then Dame Pudicity kisses my mother the virgin Vivien four times.

On the forehead.

On the chin.

On the left cheek.

And on the right.

'There,' she says. 'That is a cross of kisses.'

The abbess smiles.

'It is the way my mother used to kiss me,' she explains. 'It means may the four angels watch over you. The angel of peace. The angel of grace. The angel of holiness. And the angel of wisdom.'

'Thanks ever so,' says my mother. 'But isn't it a bit late now?'

9

Friar Blaise is long and thin and dark and cold and hard. He looks like a slate pencil, little pig. He has one eye only. That eye burns blue in his pale dry face. The other eye-socket is sewn-up, empty.

He is very interested in my mother's confession.

'Was the devil's semen hot?' he wants to know.

My mother does not understand the question, so she says nothing.

'Did the devil impregnate you with semen drawn from your father by a female succubus?' Friar Blaise asks her.

My mother seems to doubt it.

In truth, little pig, my mother the virgin Vivien cannot follow the drift of her confessor's thoughts at all, so she finds it more suitable to concentrate upon the hardness of the prieu-dieu against her kneeling knees and the agony of the man on the cross which is level with her half-shut eyes.

Friar Blaise is not deflated by his penitent's failure to respond.

'My daughter,' he says, 'we are alone. You may tell me all under the seal of the confessional. Only the truth – the whole truth – can save you now. Intercourse with demons . . . A disgusting lust!'

He draws an indefatigable breath.

'Now,' he whispers, 'let us start again.'

My mother bows her head in obedience.

The priest considers the shadowy fairness of her hair through the black lace shawl which covers her head. He can see the shape of the three neatly braided plaits.

'Are you quite ready, my child?'

'Yes, father.'

'Did the devil touch you?'

'He must have, father.'

'Your breasts, child, did he touch your breasts?'

'I don't know.'

'Did he rub your little breasts with his big member?'

'I don't think so, father. Why should he do that?'

'Was his member long? What colour was it?'

'I don't know, father. I didn't see it, father.'

Friar Blaise crosses himself. His one eye notes the dust of dandruff on my mother's shawl. It is the merest powder, like a pollen of innocence. The girl is evidently unaware of the aura of sexuality which surrounds her.

She kneels and prays, her hands pressed tight together as though she is trying to flatten a flower between them.

'My daughter,' says Friar Blaise, 'these are difficult questions, but you must concentrate.'

'I'm doing my best, father.'

'Remember everything for me.'

'There's nothing to remember. It was like a dream, a nightmare, you want to forget it.'

'Of course, of course. But the devil is a cunning husband, my child, and we must find some way to outwit him if we can. And the best way to start is to know *exactly* what happened that night you say he lay with you.'

My mother unglues her hands and studies her palms.

Oh dear, she thinks to herself, I ought to have cut my fingernails before coming to confession.

She bites the nail of the little finger of her right hand, then thinks better of it.

She puts her hands back together in a praying position, but with the nails folded inwards at the knuckles.

Here's the church, she thinks to herself –

And here's the steeple –

Open the doors – (opening her hands again) – *and* –

'Did the devil make you touch his testicles?'

'No!' – (*See all the people ...*)

'Were the devil's testicles exceedingly hairy, my child? Were they covered with thick black hair, as the blessed Saint Anthony tells us?'

'I don't know! I don't know!'

'My daughter, it is too late for prevarication, and modesty is no virtue when an immortal soul is at stake. Believe me child, it is your soul I am concerned with, not your body. Your body is no more than the dress you wear – a dress now soiled – but it is when you cast aside that dress that you will step naked in the nakedness of your everlasting soul into eternity.'

Friar Blaise rubs at his empty eye-socket with a pearlpale finger.

'Did you take the devil's organ in your mouth, my child?'

'Father!'

'Did he make you? Did he sit astride your neck and compel you to suck his member? And did he then not make you hold his testicles in your hands and press them as he came?'

'Why should he do that? Why should I do that? What has anything like that to do with my being with child by him?'

'Ah, my daughter, my daughter, I see how deep and fast the devil has you in his grasp! Now tell me. Truthfully. Thinking carefully. For the good of your immortal soul. Did you play with the devil's member?'

'No, father.'

'Did it get hard?'

'Did what get hard?'

'The devil's thing. When you played with it.'

'But I didn't play with it, I told you.'

'So it got hard without your playing with it?'

'I suppose so.'

'Without your touching it at all?'

'I don't know, father.'

'You expect me to believe that you have had intercourse with the Evil One without coming into any physical contact with his private parts?'

My mother shakes her head. Her shawl falls aside. Her face is white and distraught.

'I have never been fucked, father.'

Friar Blaise averts his one eye and crosses himself.

'I'm sorry,' says my mother. 'I know I shouldn't use words like that. I'm just trying to make it all clear to you. I know what fucking is, and it has never happened to me. Except in this dream. In this dream that I thought was a dream, but which must have been the devil, because now I am with child.'

The priest's dry rasping voice sinks again to a whisper.

'Tell me then, child, did you toss him off?'

My mother frowns.

'What is tossing off, father?'

'Much could be deduced from this,' Friar Blaise mutters to himself, 'which might be of use to Mother Church in future cases.' To the kneeling girl he says: 'Was the devil's tossed-off semen hot or freezing cold?'

'I don't know what you mean,' my mother says.

'Did you watch it trickle down your breasts?' asks Friar Blaise, a faint haze of hysteria in his voice. 'Did you observe the way that hell-born spermatozoa travelled?'

'Did *what*?'

'Rub the devil's seminal fluid into yourself? Introduce it to the secret places of your person? Lick your fingers that had grasped his horny member squirting it?'

'No!' shrieks my mother. 'No! No! No!'

'Hush, my daughter. Be at peace now. To confess all is to obtain absolution for all. Did you *swallow* his semen, my child?'

'There weren't any sea men,' says my mother.

'What?'

'There were no sailors. Hot or cold. Just the devil and me,' explains my mother.

The friar sighs.

He takes a snot-speckled handkerchief from his black sleeve and mops his brow which is pearly with perspiration.

'The devil has chosen you to be his bride,' he declares, 'either because you are exceedingly stupid or exceedingly clever. I cannot determine which.'

'Satan, thou eye, thou lust!' my mother says.

Friar Blaise blinks. 'What did you say?' he says.

'Satan,' says my mother, in the deep voice that came from her first in front of the mirror. 'Satan, thou eye, thou lust. Thou self-caused, self-determined, self-exalted, self-debased, lowest of the most high!'

Friar Blaise keeps his eye shut, as though hoping that something will go away. 'To get back to the subject of your confession,' he says with much deliberation. 'I should explain, if you are truly in such a state of ignorance, and not mocking me, your spiritual father, with wicked dissemblances and disingenuous trickeries, that when I speak of semen I speak of that filthy fluid by which the devil has transmitted (you say) the force of his evil life into your womb. I do not speak of navies.'

My mother is nodding her head, but half as if to clear it of whatever it was that lowered her voice two octaves and made her speak of Satan. 'I see,' she says at last. And then, sensibly, 'But, look, what if I *had* swallowed some of that stuff? Even the devil's? Babies don't come that way. I know that. *Do you?*'

Friar Blaise blushes.

The blush looks like rouge on his caked dry skin.

He blinks.

He lifts his hands to his face.

He looks like a man translating his thoughts into another language, and having trouble with the second tongue.

'I know lust, my child,' he says, choosing each word with a care that does not ring true. 'The lust of devils,' he goes on. 'Which surpasseth all mortal lust.'

He comes to a stop, although there seems to my mother no particular reason why he should.

He removes his pale hands from his face and considers her piously.

He crosses himself, making the sign in the Byzantine manner, from right to left with the thumb and the first two fingers held together.

'To the essentials then,' he says. 'You claim that the devil has done the deed of darkness with you?'

'Yes. I suppose so.'

'Suppose? You are not *sure*?'

'Well,' says my mother, 'I am going to have a baby. I've missed two periods. Touch of morning sickness. My breasts seem to be swelling. I must be pregnant, father. But I'm still a virgin.'

Friar Blaise leans forward suddenly and glares at her, his one eye like the tip of a red-hot poker through the grille in the confession box.

'I will speak my mind frankly now, my child,' he says. 'Amen, and so be it. What you have been telling me is arrant nonsense. Worse. It is viler than nonsense, it is blasphemy. You have come here possessed by the devil knows what wickedness – inflamed with vicious and lubricious fantasies dreamed up in your bed at night – all determined to poison the mind of a holy man doing his best to live as a Christian hermit should.'

My mother stares at him, aware that the friar is smiling all the time although what he is saying does not seem to be causeing him any amusement.

'Blasphemy is a grave sin,' Friar Blaise continues. 'Blasphemy involves contumely and dishonour towards God, and towards me as God's representative, your ghostly father. Such sins are worse than the sins of simple carnality – such as kissing the red rim of the devil's member, and running your tongue up and down it, and permitting him to insert his burning or freezing cold sexual organ up your little mouse-hole while still, by some deviltry, retaining your hymen intact.'

My mother tugs her black lace shawl back in place so that her hot cheeks cannot be seen. She hates to hear what the friar is saying.

'I am sorry, father,' she says. 'Truly, I am very sorry.'

Little pig, it is mid-day.

The priest's roses are begining to shed their petals and disclose their hearts.

The leaves of the great tree that shades his cell are curling and yellowing in the sun.

'I will do penance for my blasphemy,' my mother says. 'But all that I have said is true.'

'Impossible!'

'You can examine me, if you think so,' my mother offers.

Then she blushes beneath her black lace.

'On second thoughts,' she says, 'Dame Pudicity can examine me.'

Friar Blaise is shuddering.

He is also praying long and fast in Latin.

His eye opens very wide.

At last he says:

'Are you a witch?'

'Do I look like a witch?' says my mother.

Friar Blaise does not answer this question.

Instead, shivering, smiling but resolute, he puts his right hand on my mother's head and solemnly intones:

'I conjure you by the bitter tears shed on the cross by our saviour the Lord Jesus Christ for the salvation of the world, and by the burning tears poured in an evening hour over His wounds by the most glorious Virgin Mary, His mother, and by all the tears which have been shed here in this world by the saints and elect of God (from whose eyes He has now wiped away all tears), that if you be innocent of witchcrafts you do now shed tears, but that if you be guilty you shall by no means and in no wise do so. In the name of the Father, and of the Son, and of the Holy Ghost. Amen.'

Friar Blaise removes his hand from mother's head and wipes it on his maniple.

High above the hermit's cell a lark ascends – a pulse in the sun.

'You cannot weep!' Friar Blaise says eagerly.

'Of course I can weep,' my mother says.

'There are no tears in your eyes,' says Friar Blaise. 'Be careful now, my girl. I know the witch's trick – assuming a tearful aspect and smearing your cheeks and eyes with spittle to make it *seem* that you are weeping. God is watching you, my daughter. You'll never get away with it.'

'Fiddle de dee!' my mother says boldly. 'I weep well enough when I have something to weep about.'

'Fiddle de what?' The friar grins from ear to ear. He is furious.

'I'm sorry,' says my mother. 'I shouldn't have said that, should I? This isn't the time or the place for fiddle de dees or even tushes or pishes or rots. But it *is* rot, you know. And, father, forgive me for saying so, but what you're saying deserves something a lot worse than fiddle de dee said back at it!'

My mother considers the neatly pierced feet on the crucifix an inch before her eyes. She thinks for a moment, then she adds:

'For instance, I wept for an hour when I missed my second period. And I'd been weeping all through the woods on the way to break the news to Dame Pudicity. My face was quite red with it. You can ask her.'

'You deny then that you pinch your cheeks to make them look red from weeping? That you smear your eyelids with spittle?'

'O fiddle fiddle fiddle, and never mind the dee!' cries my mother, almost laughing. 'All, all fiddling nonsense. I can *weep* and I don't *spit* and I am not a *witch* and there were no *sailors* present of *any temperature* and not a spot or stain of your filthy fiddling *fluids*. Only the devil. And besides it was a dream.'

'A dream?'

'Like a dream,' explains my mother. She twists her hands together in the effort to make her confessor understand. 'I didn't actually *feel* anything or *see* anything or even *do* anything, don't you see? But it must have happened as I dreamt it happened, with the devil and all, because I'm going to have a baby and I have never been with a man even to sing duets and I still have my hymen intact.'

Friar Blaise recites a decade of the rosary in perfect silence. He puts his two pearlpale hands across his eye, as if to shut out the world. At last he begins to speak in a pulpit voice, the tone of which encompasses rapture and wisdom, although not necessarily in the same sentence.

'Two years ago,' he says, 'on Maundy Thursday, while I was hearing confessions at the church of the Holy Thorn at Glastonbury, a young man came to me. I am of course forbidden by holy Mother Church, in her long wisdom, from disclosing to you any of the matter of his confession. But I may remark that in the course of it he cried out in a most woeful voice, and what he cried was: "O help me, father, for I have lost my member!" I was struck all of a heap, my child. I was dumbfounded. My mental state resembled that of a duck in thunder. However, invoking the aid of the blessed Saint Pelagia the Penitent, that dancing girl at Antioch who lived disguised as a man in a cave on the Mount of Olives, I was advised not to give my penitent's complaint too easy credence, especially since in the opinion of the wise it is a mark of light-heartedness to believe too much too easily. I required my sinner, therefore, to remove his trousers. He did so. I saw. He was smooth, my child, quite smooth between the legs. I never saw such smoothness, not in eels or beeswax, even. Invoking the aid again of the blessed Saint Pelagia, I inquired of the young man whether he suspected anyone of having bewitched him to achieve this dreadful condition. And the young man said that he did indeed suspect someone, but that she was absent and living in Carlisle, by the Roman fountains. Then I said unto him: "Go to Carlisle, my son. Go to her there by the Roman fountains, and do your utmost with sweet words and deep entreaties. Go on your knees to her. Spit in your own bosom. Promise her marriage if only she will bring you again to your rightful protuberance." And the young man departed, and crawled to Carlisle, and did so. For he came back after a few weeks and he thanked me, saying that he was whole again and had recovered every part. And I believed his words, but again by the advising intercession of the blessed Saint Pelagia I proved what he told me by the evidence of my own eyes. And we gave thanks together.'

'Did he marry the witch?' says my mother.

'He did not,' says Friar Blaise.

My mother kneels, considering. She has found this a touching story, but she cannot see its relevance to her own case. She would say so, but the friar continues talking before she has a chance to formulate the thought politely. Indeed, Friar Blaise seems now to forget that they are still in the confessional, for all at once he begins preaching a sermon. His tone is melancholy, little pig. He smiles.

Friar Blaise's Sermon

'Tobias six,' announces Friar Blaise. *'The devil has power against those who are subject to their lusts.* There was a young girl in Macedonia who believed that she had been turned into a filly. Quite, quite persuaded was she, and her mother with her, and her father, and her brothers besides, and her sisters who were sober individuals, and all her many friends in Macedonia. All of these immortal souls, looking at the young girl, believed the young girl's belief – that she was a filly foal. That is to say, they saw there before them in Macedonia a filly in her shape. But the girl came before Saint Macarius the Elder, withdrawn as he was into the wilderness of Sketis, and the devil could not bewilder the senses of that decent desert monk, so that when the girl was brought before him to be healed, he perceived a true woman and not a filly foal, while on the other hand everyone else was exclaiming that she seemed to be a horse. And Macarius, by his prayers and supplications, as well as by his fastings and good works, freed the girl and her relatives and neighbours from that horse-illusion, and he proclaimed that this had happened to the girl because she had not attended sufficiently to holy things, to the life of the spirit, nor used as she should the Sacrament of Penance and the Sacrifice of the Mass. And because of this chink in the armour of her righteousness, the devil was enabled to assist a young man who desired the girl, so that when the girl would not consent to the young man's lust, the devil put it into the head of the young man to consult with a Jew who was a witch, and the Jew so bemused the girl that, by the devil's power, he turned her into a filly, apparently.

All the integrity goes out of my mother's face as she kneels listening to these words.

'I have offended God,' she cries in a tiny voice, bending her brow to touch the cold sharp grille of the confessional. 'Oh, I am ever so sorry, so sorry. My sin, my sin, my own most grievous sin.'

She strikes her breasts three times with her little clenched fist. One and a half times on each breast, my brothers.

The latticework of the grille is roughly comforting against her forehead. It leaves marks like flea-bites or stigmata.

'Mercy,' she whispers. 'Mater Mary mercy! Mater Mary mercerycordial!'

Her voice is again deep and dark as she says these words.

Friar Blaise take no notice of this new baritone outburst on the part of his penitent. Instead, he goes on with his sermon:

'The devil has power against those who are subject to their

lusts. It is so. He can injure, for his profit and his probation, the good in their fortunes – that is, in such exterior things as cash, and fame, and keeping fit. So much we learn from the case of the Blessed Job, who was most assuredly afflicted by the devil in such aspects. But these injuries of the devil's are not of the soul's causing, so that the injured may not be led or driven into any grief of sin, although they may be tempted both inwardly and outwardly in the flesh. The ultimate illusion – as of the filly foal in Macedonia – that cannot be *inflicted* upon the good by the devil, either actively or passively. Not actively, I say, by deluding the senses of the righteous as the devil deludes the senses of those others who are fallen from a state of grace. And not passively, I say, by the direct removal of their male organs by some glamour. For, consider this, and in our time, in these two respects the devil could never injure the Blessed Job – especially not by means of the passive injury with regard to the venereal act. For Job was of such continence that he was able to say: "I have vowed a vow with my eyes that I shall never think about a virgin, and still less about another man's wife." Nevertheless, dear child, my daughter, the devil knows that he has great power over sinners of all descriptions – as we see from Saint Luke eleven twenty-one: *When a strong man armed keepeth his palace, his goods are in peace.* And as we see from the parable of the farmer and his daughter who were travelling to Jericho in a wagon when they fell among thieves, and all was taken from them save some jewels that the daughter contrived to hide in her vagina. After the thieves had gone, she gave these jewels to her father, to raise his heart again. And her father said unto her: "If only your mother was here. We could have saved the horse and the wagon also." Verily then, it may be asked, as to illusions in respect of the male organ, whether, granted that the devil cannot impose this illusion in a passive way upon those in a state of grace, may he not still achieve his devilish end in a active sense upon the same graceful ones – the argument being that the man in the state of grace is prevented from the truth because his goodness makes it such that he *ought* to see his member in its right and proper place, despite the opinion of his bodily senses, as well as those of bystanders, that this same organ has been taken away from him? My child, if this great con of the devil's is conceded, why, what then? Does the world come to a stop? Time turn itself inside-out? Solomon in all his glory achieve the Sleeve Job? No. No, no, no. No in thunder! Little goose, it follows, as the night the day, that although a man in a state of grace can see the loss of another man's member – and to that extent the devil is capable of deluding the senses of the good – yet that same man in that same state of grace cannot passively suffer such loss in his own body, *since he is not subject to lust.* No lust, no loss. Fiat. In the same way, but God bless and prevent us all, the converse is true, and as the angel said unto Tobias: *Those who are given to lust, the devil has power over them.*'

Tears have formed behind my mother's tight-shut eyelids.

Now she is beginning to sob softly, banging her head against the crucifix.

'O Lord,' Friar Blaise goes on, 'but what then should be thought in all holy charity of those witches who in this devil's hobby sometimes collect male organs in great numbers, as many as twenty or thirty or thirty-five members together, and put those members in a bird's nest, or shut them up in a sewing box, where the poor abstracted things comport themselves like living fellows, and eat oats and corn like hungry horses, as has been seen by many of the saints and is a matter of common report? (For a member without a man attached has the appetite of any other creature, and needs must eat and drink to live.) I say to you, my child – calling you back by the grace of God and at the intercession of the Blessed Saint Pelagia from the devil's cozenage – if it is not indeed too late – that this, all this, is decreed and doomed and done by the devil's blasting rod and by illusion, for the senses of those who see those moving members in the sewing box are deluded in the way that I have said. For a certain man in Carbonek told me that when he had lost his member, he approached a known witch to ask her to restore it to him. The witch told the poor afflicted to climb a certain yew tree, and that he might take then whatever member he liked out of a nest in that yew tree in which there were many members. And when he tried to take the biggest one, the witch said to him: “You must not take that one.” Adding that it belonged to the priest of that parish.’

Friar Blaise reveals his eye.

‘Therefore,’ he concludes his sermon, ‘we may see how all these things are caused by the devil and shaped to his own ends by an illusion or glamour, in the manner I have described to you, by confusing the organ of vision by transmuting the mental images in the imaginative faculty. And do not believe those heretics who will tell you that the members in the nests and the sewing boxes are devils in the disguise of members, for they are not. It is true that devils sometime appear to witches in the form of assumed members, and converse with them, and perform all other manner of filthy intercourse. But they effect this glamour by an easier method – namely, by drawing out an inner mental image from the repository of the witch’s memory, and impressing it upon the surface of imagination. For, as Saint Thomas says, *Where the angel’s power is, there he operates.* Meaning by the angel, no doubt, the devil. For you must know that the devil was once the greatest angel of all, my dear, Lucifer Light-bearer, a most wicked angel, the implacable enemy and tempter of the human race, the god of this world, the *diabolos*, that artificer of sins of the flesh, to whom flesh is trash, is nothing, and who therefore can be nothing to flesh, unless indeed he be its creator and master, like God. For the devil is God, as understood by the wicked. And as Saint Paul remarks, *Satan himself is transformed into an angel of light.* So also the prophet Isaiah: *How art thou fallen from heaven, O Lucifer, son of the morning.* And finally Our Lord Himself: *I beheld Satan as lightning fall from heaven.* And thus I counsel you to think upon these things in your heart, and to watch and pray, and to fear the day of judgement, and to be in dread of hell. In the name of the Father, and of the Son, and of the Holy Ghost.’

‘Amen,’ says my mother.

And the tears run down her stricken cheeks and splash against her hands that claw the grille.

Friar Blaise’s eye considers her with brusque compassion. ‘It can be said,’ he observes, ‘that the grace of tears is one of the chief gifts allowed to the penitent, for Saint Bernard tells us that the tears of the humble can penetrate to heaven and conquer the unconquerable.'

'And I am *not* a witch!' sobs my mother. 'My tears prove it, don't they? I may be a beastly pregnant virgin and guilty of blasphemy thereby, but *I am not a witch*!'

Friar Blaise lowers his eye.

He sighs. He smiles.

'It can sometimes suit the devil's cunning,' he says, 'to allow even a witch to weep. With God's permission, of course.'

'Why?' cries my mother. 'Why? Why? Why?'

'Since tearful grieving, weaving, and deceiving are said to be proper to women,' Friar Blaise observes. 'However,' he concedes, 'we may postpone any further consideration of that until tomorrow. Yes, child, until after you have been examined by the abbess. Meanwhile, pray.'

My mother's voice drops once more unbidden to a lower register, and words tumble out of her mouth:

'*Adonai, Zeboth, Adon, Schadai, Elion, Tetragrammaton, Eloi, Elohim, Messias . . .*'

'Prayer is not a noise,' says Friar Blaise.

'Then I don't know how, father, I don't know what – '

'Prayer is perfect,' says Friar Blaise, 'when we pray without knowing to whom we pray.'

All the same, and to my mother's great surprise, he gives her penance and absolution.

He blesses her. He stops smiling.

And then he winks.

10

Behold! I am yesterday. Behold! I am today. Behold! I am the enemy of tomorrow and O Satan, thou eye, thou lust, *Adonai, Zeboth, Adon, Schadai, Elion, Tetragrammaton . . .*

It's all go, brothers mine.

I hope – in other words – you realized?

I am the deep voice speaking in my mother.

11

(1) The Sleeve Job.
(2) Diana's manor.
(3) The brachet chasing the hart and the fifty black hounds chasing the brachet.
(4) Free will.
(5) YHVH.
(6) The lance of Longinus.
(7) Who is writing this book?
(8) Male members in sewing boxes, etc.
(9) The sword in the stone.
(10) The nature of evil.
(11) The right question to ask the Holy Grail.
(12) My birth and deaths.
(13) King Arthur and the knights of the Round Table.

These are some other things that I'll be coming to.

12

Dame Pudicity's cell is sparsely furnished.

An earthenware jug.

A wooden table.

A statue of the Blessed Virgin Mary, complete with snake spurned underfoot.

A crucifix.

An iron bed with a black paillasse.

A scourge of birch twigs hanging from a hook.

Entering the room of the abbess in fear, alone, at night, my mother the virgin Vivien notices nothing else at first. Later she will be made aware of other accoutrements, but her original and lasting impression is of austerity.

The wind howls through the long corridors and whispers in the secret recesses of the convent of the Flaming Heart.

The hour is between Matins and Lauds.

'Friar Blaise has sent me to you,' says my mother, 'for a reason which I think you know.'

Her voice approximates to a boldness which she does not feel.

She kisses Dame Pudicity's ring.

The abbess says nothing in response. Instead, she inclines her head the merest fraction, acknowledging that she does indeed understand the purpose of this nocturnal tryst, and moves with a cool swish of her long white robes to light two candles before the statue of the Virgin and then to kneel in prayer.

My mother says:

'It is amazing to me that the friar thinks this necessary. I was taught to believe that truth is self-evident to the good.'

The abbess, at her orisons, ignores her.

My mother, guilty at having chattered aloud her falsely impudent thoughts, all as a mask for the fear which possesses her heart, now throws herself down on her knees beside the white-robed figure.

Dame Pudicity does not even favour her with a sidelong glance. The abbess is up on her own feet again the instant that my mother's knees touch the bare stone floor. She paces the cell in swift agitation of spirit.

'What is it?' my mother asks her.

The abbess looks everywhere save at the young girl kneeling.

'The hanged man,' she mutters, kicking out at the hemline of her habit.

'Beg pardon?' says my mother.

'The tower struck by lightning,' says Dame Pudicity, without a pause in her pacing. 'The fool. The female Pope. Amaranthus.'

'But what does Amaranthus mean?' says my mother.

'Oh, holy light, probably,' says the abbess in a way that suggests that it doesn't.

'I see,' says my mother. Then she says:

'No. I don't see. What on earth are you talking about?'

The abbess stops in her pacing.

She is standing beneath the cell's single window, which is high and functional – designed for the ingress of light and air, and not to afford any view to beguile the eyes of the cell's inmate.

Moonlight streams down around her in a single column from this window, making her robes the more white by its whiteness. Her eyes are green in the shadow of her coif as she gazes up a moment at the high stone walls. It seems to occur to her that the light of the moon, even coupled as it is with the flickering flames of the candles she has lit before the statue of the Virgin, might be insufficient for the illumination of her room. She takes four rushlight torches and ignites them, placing one at each corner of the iron bed, where they burn like four blue and flaming fists upraised. When the act is completed, she says: 'I am talking about witchcraft, my child.'

My mother frowns. 'How boring.'

'*Boring?*' shrieks the abbess. 'What's boring about the Keys of Solomon and the *Grimoriun Verum* and the *Osculum Infame*?'

'I can't speak any foreign languages,' my mother says, putting one finger in her rosebud of a mouth.

Dame Pudicity swings around and stares at her in the torch-light.

'The Infamous Kiss,' she hisses. 'Kissing the devil's backside.'

'That sounds nasty,' says my mother, pouting the rosebud, and plucking at it with her finger.

'Nastiness isn't in it,' insists the abbess. 'I am talking about such vileness and putrescence of mind and body and spirit as the rational soul will scarcely credit. I'm talking about the crucifixion of toads and washing your mandrake every Friday evening with red wine and keeping it wrapped in your mother's shroud.'

My mother tosses her hair. It is like spun gold in the light of the four torches, with richer deeper shadows where the moon-light falls across it.

'Isn't it all nonsense really?'

'*Nonsense?*' The abbess of the convent of the Flaming Heart springs back as though insulted. 'Is the black cock nonsense? Its hideous heart? Its tongue that crows even when it has been plucked out? The first feather of its left wing which can write a letter to make a cancer in the eyes of those that read it? Is Apollyon nonsense? Or Belial?'

My mother has no notion of how to begin answering such questions, so she keeps her mouth shut. The nun, for her part, seems hardly to notice that her visitor has fallen silent. She moves about busily at the table. She opens its drawer and takes out a platter. She pours water into the platter from the earthenware jug, and rubs herbs against her hand, making a lather. As she performs these tasks, she goes on chattering:

'There's rosemary – that's for remembrance, and to keep away the nightmare too. Rue – *Ruta graveolens*, which hinders lust. A roebuck's gall – which doesn't. Powder from the horn of the African rhinoceros . . .'

She bites her lips, and looks sharply at my mother. 'You realize what I'm doing?'

'Making a lather in a platter,' mother says. 'Do nuns have to shave then?'

Dame Pudicity looks down with embarrassment at the white mess in the palm of her left hand. 'Not this,' she says hurriedly. 'I mean did you realize what I was just saying? Did you notice that everything I mentioned began with R?'

My mother shakes her head in helpless bewilderment. A strand of yellow hair falls across her cheek, as innocent as a catkin dangling.

The abbess titters.

'Good,' she says. 'Never mind that then.'

Her soft green eyes consider Vivien from top to toe.

'Now,' she says, 'I want you to take off your dress.'

'Take off my dress?' says my mother.

'Yes, child. And any other little things you happen to be wearing.'

The abbess says this so pleasantly, and with such crisp matter-of-factness, that my mother finds herself in a state of enchanted compliance.

She slips her dress over her head, and takes off her linen underskirt, her sandals, and her two bracelets.

After a moment's hesitation, she draws the silver pins from her hair also, and runs her finger through the braids, tossing her head so that all that golden glory tumbles free about her shoulders.

The nun has turned her back while this undressing was completed.

Still without looking round, she says:

'Lie down. On the bed.'

'Lie down?' says my mother.

'On your back,' the abbess orders.

'But why?' demands my mother.

'You will do as I say, child.'

The nun's tone brooks no disagreement.

Mother lies down, little wolf.

Dame Pudicity turns.

She looks at the naked girl.

My mother is lying on her back on the iron bed. Her body is white against the black paillasse. Her hair streams about her shoulders but cannot conceal the snowy mounds of her breasts, each tipped with a nipple like a little pink flower.

Four torches flare at the iron bed's corners.

My mother's hands are covering her sex.

'Take your hands away from there,' commands the abbess.

My mother blushes.

'My father will kill me . . .'

'Do as I say!'

My mother removes first one hand, then the other.

The nun's eyes are like stars on a frosty night. Disgust and fascination caress each other in her regard of the young girl's body.

My mother's pubic region is downed with soft gold hair.

She smiles up nervously at her examiner.

'What are you going to do to me?' she asks.

The abbess crosses herself.

Little pig, you can see the trembling of her breasts beneath her robe.

The lather is dripping from her extended left hand, O Jesus.

'I am going to shave you,' she says.

'*Shave* me?' says mother. 'What for?'

Dame Pudicity favours her with a chaste smile. The unnatural brightness is fading from her eyes. A moment ago they blazed with the lucidity of three stars. Now they more resemble green pools where rings or other minor trinkets lie lost but glinting in the dusky depths.

'Their face is as a burning wind, and their voice the hissing of serpents,' the abbess says.

Her voice has a shiver in it.

She kneels down by the bedside in the light of the four flaming torches.

'Inquire, inquire,' says she, beginning to lather my mother's mound of Venus. 'All the kingdoms of this world have been overthrown by women. Troy, that great town of towers, destroyed, and many brothers slain. The wanton's name was Helen.' The abbess is making a considerable foam between my mother's legs. 'The kingdom of the Jews,' she goes on, 'ruined by Jezebel and her daughter Athaliah, Queen of Judah, who caused her son's sons to be killed, that on their death she might reign herself.'

My mother opens her rosebud mouth to comment.

'*Improbe amor*,' says the abbess, lathering, lathering, '*quid non mortalia pectora cogis?*'

My mother shuts her mouth again.

Dame Pudicity is taking a razor from a black bag tied to the girdle of her robe. It is an excellent razor, of thin sharp steel, with an ivory handle.

Dame Pudicity is producing a leather strop from around her thigh. She wears the strop as a garter.

The abbess strops the razor.

She tests its keenness upon a strand of her own hair, extracted from the coif.

She spreads her fingers skilfully in the foam between my mother's thighs, and begins to shave the virgin of her pubic hair.

'According to Cato of Utica,' she says conversationally, '*If the world could be rid of women, we should not be without God in our intercourse.*'

My mother is saying nothing.

She finds the razor tickly, but also nice.

Soon the strange abbess of the convent of the Flaming Heart has shaved every inch of the area around the young girl's sexual parts.

13

My brothers, an eye is watching.

Observing all this.

A blue eye.

A cold eye.

An eye like a sapphire.

Colder than sapphire.

An eye like lapis lazuli.

Blue stone silicate.

Like lapis lazuli also in that there is a vein of sulphur in it.

Look:

Pressed to the spyhole in the ceiling of the cell.

An eye, O Jesukin.

Cold.

Blue.

Bright.

Unblinking.

Little pig, it is Friar Blaise.

That monk is crouched hidden in a secret alcove above Dame Pudicity's cell. Entrance to this chamber, to be had from a concealed staircase behind the cloisters, is known only to himself and the abbess. The place is no bigger than a cupboard. But a cupboard big enough for a man to kneel in.

Friar Blaise is kneeling now.

He is in that extreme prayerful position known as prostration, favoured by the Carthusian monks of Saint Bruno, kneeling so that his tonsured head is bent forward flat against the ground in front of him.

O Christ, he is not praying.

The spyhole is drilled directly above the iron bed.

The four torches burn like bridal lamps.

Friar Blaise has a perfect view.

14

'*Donne*,' says the abbess, who studied in Rome as a young nun, '*donne, asini e noci voglion le mani atroci.*' She is wiping the remaining suds of shaving soap from her fingers. 'Now, I want you to open your knees wide.'

My mother does as she is told.

'Wider,' says the abbess. 'Like opening the pages of a book out flat.'

My mother does her best to comply. She lies staring up at the whiteness of the cell's ceiling, where one fly seems established right above her. The iron bed is hard beneath her bottom.

'Shut your eyes, child,' says Dame Pudicity.

My mother obeys – but not before she has caught a glimpse of the abbess kilting up her robes, and observed through half-closed eyelashes the flash of pale legs as Dame Pudicity joins her on the black paillasse.

Now my mother is feeling the light brush of fingers in her groin.

She giggles.

'That's ticklish,' she says. 'Just where you've shaved me,' she apologizes. 'It's a bit sensitive.'

'Be at peace, girl,' the nun says in a stern voice. 'I'm not asking you to do anything. Just lie completely still.'

My mother can feel the fingers of the abbess tracing round and round the lips of her newly bald vagina.

The experience is so strange that she has to bite her tongue to stop herself from laughing.

Then she bites her tongue again.

Much harder.

Because that nun's clever fingers are pressing upon the little bud at the top of her love parts.

Pressing, old wolf my friend.

And playing with it.

Playing with the part which my mother herself has only recently discovered, in the darkness of her bed at home, as a source of pleasure and comfort when sleep will not come.

My mother cannot control or comprehend the lovely liquescent drowning sensations spreading in deep and deeper ripples from the rubbing of the nun's attentive fingers. She wants to cry out. She feels a great urge to thrust her whole body up off the bed, and get the brisk cause of this pleasure right inside her.

She wants to weep.

She wants to laugh.

She wants to kiss the hand that is bringing her such sweetness and such fire.

Instead, obediently, my mother keeps quite quiet and still.

Now, little pig.

Oh, my Jesus.

Now those playing fingers are seeking entrance to her.

My mother can feel one of them at it.

Hard and sharp. Cunning. Elegant. Pointed.

Then –

Now –

That finger is inside.

Pressing, little pig.

Prodding, little pig.

Poking, little pig.

Delicious barbs of pleasure.

My young mother has never before experienced such pleasure as she is getting from what this busy finger is doing to her love parts.

Now it stops.

Then it starts again.

Stops again.

Starts again.

Little wolf, that finger seems to know just what to do.

It stops just long enough for my mother to rest – then to need it to go on again more than anything she has ever known or needed in the world.

And each time it stops it starts again with a tickly and assiduous and enterprising difference of attack that makes my mother think that another finger is inside her, a finger with different ideas, another sort of diligence, sedulous, stirring, so that the young girl is being rubbed up, now this way, now that, until her whole vagina feels like a little sucking whirlpool wound round and round by the whim of gravity and the wind and the meeting of currents of feeling that my mother never dreamt of.

The abbess of the convent of the Flaming Heart is evidently skilled in this art of examining virgins.

But –

'. . . Oh!'

My mother screams.

Little pig, she cannot stop herself.

Screaming.

For now what Dame Pudicity is doing is hurting her.

My mother feels torn.

Lacerated, little pig.

Ravaged.

Opened up, O Jesus.

'Lie still, lie quiet,' says the nun soothingly, cooingly. 'It's only my fingers, only my little fingers . . .'

My mother screams louder.

'No!' she cries. 'You can't, I tell you! I mean – not *two* fingers! And not like that! You can't go right in . . . You can't, you mustn't, you just can't!'

She opens her eyes wide and thrusts herself up on one elbow.

She sees Dame Pudicity kneeling between her opened legs.

The nun's face is hot and flushed. Her wimple has come adrift. It trails across the black paillasse.

Wriggling sideways, my mother is able to see that her tutor has been trying to get two fingers into her vagina. The abbess has very fine and slender fingers, but the attempt is proving impossible.

Dame Pudicity stands up abruptly and pulls down her white silk robes.

'I see,' she says.

My mother is missing that probing finger.

She tries to catch Dame Pudicity's hand and kiss it.

She wants that one finger back where it has been.

Not two, little pig.

Her virgin slot cannot accommodate two fingers.

But her love parts ache and itch with the frustration of the feelings engendered there by the nun's one-fingered frigging.

Dame Pudicity snatches her hand away. She will not let the girl kiss it.

'I see,' she says again, in an uncompromising voice.

Friar Blaise sees too, O little Jesus, with his one cold and burning eye, pressed tight against the spyhole in the floor of the secret alcove above.

The monk has watched as my mother was shaved.

He saw her lie flat on her back directly below him on the iron bed.

He observed everything as Dame Pudicity climbed into position between the young girl's legs spread out like the pages of an opened book.

He enjoyed a perfect view as the nun played first gently and then quite fiercely with my mother's little love bud, his eye moving backwards and forth between the playing hand and the expression on my mother's face.

He noted the gradual smile of ecstasy that came there.

He heard the quick gasps and involuntary exhalations of delight that escaped from my mother's excited lips.

He held his breath as Dame Pudicity tried the assault with two thrusting fingers.

He saw the abbess get off the bed and pull down her skirts.

He observed the girl's attempts to get that exciting hand returned to work between her legs.

And now Friar Blaise is still watching as my mother lies back panting on the black paillasse on the iron bed. He can see that her eyes are glazed and that her nipples are stiff with anticipation. He is observing the uncontrollable shivers and tremblings that run through her virgin body. Her right hand is hovering over her shaven love parts. Her right hand is plunging to comfort herself there as soon as Dame Pudicity's back is turned.

Friar Blaise watches as my mother the virgin Vivien plays with herself.

But Vivien is inexperienced and performs the act of masturbation clumsily, and the voyeur friar can see that she is nowhere near her climax as the abbess approaches the bed again.

15

'Capperi! Cappita!' says the abbess, with languid gaiety. 'We have established that you are a virgin. We have still to establish whether or not you are a witch.'

My mother is far too excited to protest her innocence of witchcraft. Her forefinger still moves about its task of self-stimulation.

Dame Pudicity watches her for a moment. The nun's exquisite face – with its look of having been chiselled out of white marble by craftsman's hands in patient adoration – wears a new expression.

'You're not so good at that,' she says.

And she grins like a fox eating shit out of a wire brush.

My mother blushes. She stops.

'Scratch, scratch, scratch,' the nun says critically. 'You're like a bloody cat.'

Her own hands move busily in another earthenware bowl. She is shaking in ingredients from various small bottles and querns produced from the pockets of her robes, and from the drawer in the wooden table.

'You should do it as though you are playing an instrument,' the abbess goes on. 'It's like making music. It *is* making music in yourself, when you come to think of it.'

My mother has turned her face to the wall. 'To be nothing,' she says. 'To be a fish born from a thorn.' She scratches at her bare throat with her hand, for her voice has once more dropped unaccountably into a lower octave. *'O Tarot,'* she is saying. *'O Nizael, Estarnas, Xatros.'*

She shakes her head, unable to understand the sounds that issue from herself. At the same time, she is feeling embarrassed and frustrated. She is rubbing her thighs together in an involuntary spasm of desire.

The abbess looks at her with an interest which amounts

almost, but not quite, to tenderness. For a moment it is as if she might respond to my mother in the same strange tongue. She does not. The moment passes.

My mother is picking at the black paillasse with irritable fingers. Now she kisses it with her neat little rosebud mouth, self-mockingly. When she speaks again it is in her natural voice, sweet and fluting, looking up sidelong at Dame Pudicity with her cheek half-caressing itself against the black stuff, and her eyes ablaze with a provocative sarcasm.

'I'm sure you could do it better, couldn't you?' my mother is saying. 'Nuns have to, don't they? Nuns must be the best – the best – the best – ' (My mother is groping for the word she does not know.)

'Masturbators,' says the abbess of the convent of the Flaming Heart, pestle in hand, mixing.

'Nuns must be the best masturbators in the world, I suppose,' my mother says.

Friar Blaise snorts.

He is, of course, still watching from above.

He does not care for this slur on the honour of monks.

The friar's hand gropes under his cassock for his cock.

It would be apt and satisfactory to wank now, he thinks to himself, with this fifteen-year-old virgin stretched out on the bed for his secret delectation.

Alas, my brothers, he finds that the position in which he is kneeling – with his head pressed right down against the floor to give his eye access to the spyhole – does not allow him to hold his member in his hand without losing sight of the scene below.

And to relinquish sight of that scene is more than Friar Blaise could bear at this moment.

Even for the sake of a necessary and no doubt delicious orgasm.

Even to uphold the reputation of his Order.

Reluctantly, therefore, the monk lets his prick hang loose and unrubbed.

All the same.

Yes, little pig.

All the same, even in an unrubbed state, it gets as hard as an iron bar as he watches what happens next.

16

'Vivien,' says Dame Pudicity.

'Yes?'

'Let me show you how,' the nun says softly.

She giggles like a schoolgirl.

She writhes a little in her white silk robes.

Then she lifts her robes and exposes her sex.

She is quite naked under the habit.

My mother, fascinated, watches with big blue eyes.

(The eye above is watching too.)

First, the abbess removes from the third finger of her right hand the gold ring with an amethyst set in it, which is part of her insignia.

She gives the ring to my mother, with a coquettish smile, slipping it on the third finger of the young girl's right hand instead.

Now Dame Pudicity moistens all four fingers of her right hand on her own lips, and puts them down between her legs.

She starts to rub.

She rubs lightly at first, wistfully, in a slow and even tempo, tickling herself, barely touching the lips of her vagina.

Now the rubbing becomes more vigorous.

O Christ, more urgent.

She has her clitoris firmly in hand and she is giving it no mercy.

Her fingers dance.

Her fingers pinch.

Her fingers pull.

Her fingers spank.

My mother is amazed at how *big* the nun's clitoris seems to be growing.

She can't take her eyes off it.

The abbess can't take her fingers off it.

My mother is remembering also what Dame Pudicity said a moment ago about doing this properly being like playing a musical instrument. The nun's pale and ethereal oval face does indeed seem concentrated now on some absolute and far-away music which is playing for her ears only.

She looks, indeed, to be fast approaching a state of transcendent bliss.

But no.

Now she stops.

Now she is groaning, the tall abbess, and she is crossing her shapely aristocratic legs upon her own hand where it is thrust.

But the nun's exquisite masturbatory pleasure is far from complete – for after a moment of standing thus, panting, amorous, dishevelled, as if by an act of deliberate concentration and self-control she is withholding the moment of longed-for final release, Dame Pudicity draws out her fingers slowly, self-teasingly, and then presses down hard with her whole genital area, face down, pelvis down, thrusting, wriggling, thumping and drumming herself against the frame of the iron bed.

With a soft moan, she is inserting her fingers into her vagina.

She pokes.

She thrusts.

She bucks, rolling over on her back and jerking up and down happily.

Her movements now are jumpy and skittish and unpredictable, her body like a white lamb playing in the spring sunshine, kicking and frolicking, doing what it likes when it likes.

Soon the nun has her other hand up under her habit also, playing with her own nipples.

Her face is ecstatic.

Her cheeks are like red roses.

Her eyes are burning.

Finally her needs become too much for her. She has tantalized and teased and caressed herself to the point of no return.

Dame Pudicity, abbess of the convent of the Flaming Heart, is sinking slowly to the stone floor of the cell, and reaching for a candle from the rack of votive candles burning before the statue of the Blessed Virgin Mary.

She seizes a candle in one hand, while her other hand works busily at her cunt.

She is pinching out the burning candle between finger and

thumb, with an indifference to the flame which my mother can only suppose must derive from the waves of pleasure surging through her body convulsively and making her heedless of anything save her own erotic needs.

And now the abbess is lying on her back, her white robes up as high as her breasts, her eager thighs pumping up and down with soft wet sucking sounds as she is pushing the candle in and out of her cunt, using both hands at once, working over her vagina and clitoris with hands and candle, candle and hands, pleasuring herself again and again and again with penetrating thoroughness and efficiency.

She comes.

She comes utterly silently – the fruit no doubt of long and lonely years of discipline and practice, thinks my mother.

But from the beatific beauty of her face, and the profound satisfaction implicit in her shuddering breathing, my mother knows precisely when each peak of climax is coming to the nun.

And she sees that it is good.

'*Deo Gratias,*' Dame Pudicity says matter-of-factly.

Then she stands up, smooths down her robes, takes her ring back from my mother and replaces it on the third finger of her own right hand, relights the candle and puts it back in position in the votive rack, and returns to her pestling.

'It's lovely,' she says in the same neutral voice as she works over the mixture in the earthenware bowl. 'Sometimes, my dear, sometimes I think that frigging yourself is the loveliest thing in the world – apart from prayer and the blessed Sacrifice of the Mass, of course.'

All at once, there is lightning and a clap of thunder in the night sky directly above the convent of the Flaming Heart.

A bell in the tower starts ringing as if pulled by demons, or by the lightning itself, or by the vibrations which the thunder has set up in the ancient stones.

Another bell begins.

And then a third.

The bells all jangling hideously out of tune.

Out of time.

Without meaning.

Without music.

The sound is to my mother's ears like a satanic parody of the ringing of bells that marks the elevation of the host. It is as if a priest has suddenly gone mad in the midst of Mass and interspersed the consecration of the elements with blasphemies.

My mother shakes with fear. Overcome with shame, she covers her naked sex with her hands and tries to hide herself in the black paillasse.

But Dame Pudicity takes no notice.

To her, it is as if there is no storm at all, as if she hears no thunder, sees no lightning, is not in the least disturbed by the meaningless ringing of the bells.

And, as suddenly as it began, it is over.

No storm, little pig. No bells, little wolf.

Only the sound of Dame Pudicity busy with her pestle in the earthenware bowl.

So that my mother wonders if it has ever been?

Or if it was all in her head?

She shudders.

She shivers.

She crosses herself.

Dame Pudicity turns round. The mixture is evidently ready. She carries it aloft before her, holding the bowl in both hands, coming towards the bed. walking slowly and with care.

'And now,' she is saying, 'now we shall see if you are really a little witch.'

17

The abbess takes a handful of the mixture and slaps it none too gently on to my mother's flesh, just below her breasts.

She begins to rub it in.

She massages up and she massages down.

She is rubbing more and more into the shaven genital areas, and plenty also over the mounds which speak of my mother's incipient womanhood.

The abbess is paying particular attention to my mother's

breasts. Her slender skilful fingers work in several slaps of the mixture.

My mother, after the initial shock, has given herself up to enjoying the massage.

There is something especially piquant, it occurs to her, in being so rubbed by fingers which she has just lately observed in the act of rubbing their owner's sex.

Dame Pudicity's hands still give off a delicious odour of her own love juices – but my mother is too young and inexperienced to be recognizing this. Instead, she is noticing only the strong nectarine smell of the unguent which is being applied to her firm white flesh.

'What is it?' she inquires.

The nun does not answer.

No, my Jesukin.

She crooks her forefinger in the thickest part of the mixture instead, and now she is thrusting finger and sticky ointment right up my mother's cunt.

18

Dame Pudicity's anointing oil contains:

the dew of white rose petals,
sandalwood,
frankincense,
violets,
liquor of saffron,
the seed of black poppies,
gum benjamin,
cinquefoil,
coriander,
henbane,
juice of hemlock,
lavender,
goldenrod –

all liquefied in oil of amber and red wine.

The result she believes to be a potent elixir in aiding the

discovery of a witch. Indeed, if you ask her she will tell you that it has never failed. Although you can't just rub it into the private parts of the suspected witch and then sit back and wait.

19

The anointing over, Dame Pudicity is taking bodkins from her pocket. The bodkins gleam silver in the torchlight. They are thick and sharp, with large eyes, the sort of pins used for drawing tapes through hems.

Before my mother can stop her, the nun begins pricking her breasts and belly, a bodkin in each hand.

My mother squeals. 'That hurts!'

'Are you sure?' inquires Dame Pudicity.

'*Sure?* It's terrible! Stop! *Please!*'

The abbess gives the left breast one final prick, as if to make it incontestable that her victim is telling the truth.

'Look,' complains my mother, 'it's bleeding where you pricked me.'

'That is good,' says Dame Pudicity.

My mother is cleaning herself with straw plucked from the paillasse. 'You make me bleed all over my belly and breasts,' she cries, 'and you say it's good. What's good about it?'

'Witches don't bleed,' says the abbess authoritatively. 'Or, if they do, the elixir makes them burn so much that they confess their wickedness.'

My mother shrugs her shoulders.

'I'm bloody bleeding and not bloody burning,' she says, with a laconic modesty. 'It just seems a pity that neither you nor Friar Blaise believed me without having to go through all this performance.'

Mention of the name of Friar Blaise makes the abbess give a little start. If she has forgotten his presence in the upper chamber, she certainly remembers it now. The reminder that her intimate inquisition of the young girl has been watched all the while by the one-eyed monk serves as a fresh inspiration to the strange nun's ingenuity.

She strides to the wall and takes down from the hook the scourge fashioned of birch twigs.

'Roll over,' she says.

'Why?' asks my mother.

'I'll give you why,' snaps Dame Pudicity. 'Discipline! That's what you need, my girl!'

My mother is frightened, little apple tree, my sweetness.

The nun cuts at the air with the birch scourge.

'You do what I say,' she commands in a shrill voice, 'or it will be the worse for you!'

There is something oddly bird-like about her, my mother notices. But the situation does not allow for protracted reflection as to the species of bird. With a sigh of fear and resignation, my mother does as she has been told. She rolls over on the paillasse so that her stomach and her private parts, her poor pricked breasts and her thighs still all smeared with the sticky sweet unguent are pressing down into the adamancy of the iron bed.

In this position, my mother's bottom makes an irresistible target for the scourge.

Dame Pudicity does not hesitate.

She likes these kinds of situations.

Her arm comes up, and the birch with it.

Her arm comes down.

Smack.

And up again.

And down again.

Smack.

Smack.

Smack.

My mother is being lightly but thoroughly beaten on her bare white bum.

As before, with Friar Blaise in the confessional that noon, my mother finds an unstoppable urge to penitence welling up inside her. She has done nothing specifically wrong that she can think of. Nothing that was really her own fault, when you come to look at it dispassionately. All the same, she is possessed by feelings of sorrow and contrition, as though the act of punishment itself is calling forth in her the memory of some aboriginal calamity, some crime, some essential sin she could not name and without doubt has never personally committed. And so strong are these feelings of guilt that my mother wishes Dame Pudicity would whip her harder, harder, to drive them out, yes, and also because she seems to need the whipping.

'Oh I am so sorry, so sorry, so very very sorry!'

My mother is sobbing.

The birch rises and falls.

The birch rises again and falls again, harder, sharper, as the thrashing abbess warms to her work of chastisement, a work in which she has grown expert, having had for the whipping the naked buttocks of so many disobedient little novices.

'My sin!' cries my mother. 'My sin, my sin, my sin!'

While a lower voice, the deeper second voice in her womb, is crying: 'Go down, Lucifer!'

(Me, O Jesukin.)

Dame Pudicity, though, is too excited now to hear or take heed of that second voice. She whips and whips. She can't stop whipping.

And the eye pressed hard to the hole above grows colder and brighter as my mother's well-whipped bottom grows as red as a strawberry with the marks of the birch.

And now there is no eye, but milk or snow or manna falling in a creamy shower from the hole, and splashing on to my mother's blushing buttocks.

My mother, weeping, gasping, threshing in a confused ecstasy of feelings which are new to her, does not heed or notice what is raining down upon her person.

The abbess, however, observes the white stains.

She stops her whipping.

She is looking up at the hole and she is smiling.

And now she is kneeling and kissing that hot snow where it has fallen.

20

'And Sir Perceval,' says the devil my father, 'rode on until he came to a valley, through which a river ran. And the borders of the valley were thick with woods, with level meadows on both sides of the river. And on one side of the river he saw a flock of white sheep, and on the other side a flock of black sheep. And when a white sheep bleated a black sheep would cross the river and turn white, and when a black sheep bleated a white sheep would cross the river and turn black. And Sir Perceval saw a tall tree by the side of the river, and one half of the tree was in flames from the root to the top, and the other half of the tree was green with leaves.'

21

'And Sir Perceval grinned,' say my uncle Astarot and my uncle Beelzebub together, 'Sir Perceval grinned like a fox eating shit out of a wire brush.'

22

Friar Blaise looks chastened.

'More goes on here,' he says, 'than meets the eye.'

My mother, in her shaggy crimson cloak, is kneeling once again before him in his cell.

'I am not a witch,' she whispers. 'You believe me now?'

'I believe you.'

'And that I am a virgin? The abbess told you so?'

'The abbess gave an excellent report of you,' the friar says briefly.

'But I *am* pregnant,' says my mother.

'So it appears.'

'And the devil is the father of my child.'

'So you say.'

'I'm telling the truth.'

Friar Blaise sighs. 'It could be true,' he concedes. 'I knew a girl once in Colchester . . .'

His voice trails raspingly away as he lets the thought go.

'No matter,' he resumes. 'The case is irrelevant. Yours, though, child, has unique features.'

He is silent a moment, the good friar, reflecting.

My mother says: 'I told my father and he has thrown me out. He called me names. He said I was the devil's whore. And worse.'

'What could be worse than that?'

My mother crosses herself.

'He said my baby would be the Antichrist.'

The friar smiles.

'That is what they propose, I dare say.'

'Who?'

'The powers of darkness,' explains Friar Blaise. 'They plan your child as the Antichrist – the antidote to what Our Lord has achieved in saving the world from everlasting perdition. As a start, do you see, they have by some means got you pregnant while you yet remain, in a technical sense, a virgin. It is a fiendish plot.'

My mother nods. 'So it is,' she agrees, catching on fast, 'for arch fiends plotted it.'

The friar's eye gleams for a moment as clear and blue as the *caelum* in the bottom of an alchemist's retort.

'God has other faces,' he observes. 'While there's life there's – '

He seems unable to finish the simple remark, so my mother helps him:

'Hope?' she suggests.

'Mmm. Something of that too,' Friar Blaise says enigmatically.

Then he falls to fingering his rosary without saying anything.

The monk seems very old and tired today, my mother thinks. Also he looks at something of a loss for an object for his words and thoughts, like an actor suddenly without an audience.

The next time my mother peeps through the grille she sees that her confessor has fallen asleep.

Worse, dear darling daughter.

He is snoring and muttering to himself.

'There is ... in God ... some say ... a deep but dazzling darkness ...'

'Holy Mary Mother of God,' moans my poor mother, abandoned in herself, 'mystical rose, tower of ivory, house of gold, queen of virgins – I shall be nothing. I shall be cast down and flagellated for ever in hell by whole schools of avenging nuns. To be the mother of the Antichrist – Lord God, what did I do, what did I ever do to deserve this?'

My mother is all at once quite overcome with supernatural terrors, thinking of the evil property in her womb.

'Oh, oh, star of the morning, mother most pure, mother most chaste, mother inviolate, mother undefiled – '

With crisping hands and heaving little breasts –

'I am lost!' cries my mother the virgin Vivien. 'Oh, I am lost. Lost! Lost!'

'Not so,' says Friar Blaise, abruptly awake again.

His eye shines like the sky-blue stone.

'Nothing is ultimately lost,' he goes on. 'Now listen carefully, child. I have dreamed a dream.'

23

'Fuck this,' says my father. 'He has dreamed a dream.'

The devil seizes a star and hurls it into the abyss.

'I abase myself before you on your little golden pot,' says my uncle Beelzebub. 'I'm sorry, but I fear it was my fault.'

My uncle Astarot is drinking mescal. 'The bit I liked,' he says, 'the bit I really liked was that conversation in the confessional. Making the friar say all that about kissing it and sucking it and did you swallow it and was it hot.'

'He was *thinking* it,' says my uncle Beelzebub modestly.

'They always do,' my father confirms, watching the star's progress.

'But to make the old eunuch *say* it,' says my uncle Astarot. He is holding up his goblet in a toast, half in honour of the prince's possession of Friar Blaise. 'Here's to the kisses I've snatched, and the snatches I've kissed!' My uncle Astarot smacks his lips. 'The beauty of this,' he says, 'the beauty of this is that we are making them say it and do it.' He pours himself another shot of mescal. 'I like this making people,' he concludes.

The star freezes. Now it is no more than one of the tears on the face of a soul in the ninth circle.

'Dreams,' says my father, 'I do not like.'

'Cosmocrator, I have apologized,' says uncle B.

Count Astarot regards his fellow devil through the lens of the mescal. Beelzebub hums and buzzes, at work among the fly-pots. He wears his customary ginger boots and his doublet of silver brocade. Something in the tilt of his head suggests an alchemist bending over a retort. Astarot knows that his colleague's body is more or less covered with hair, but as is the case with most of his creatures, the diptera, this hairy covering is so short that to the unaided eye the prince's face appears bare. His colour is blue. Astarot sees through the mescal that the long slit of Beelzebub's mouth is smiling, which means he is not happy.

'That sermon about the bird's nest full of pricks,' says uncle A. 'Great stuff. First rate theology. What crap.'

'Straight out of the *Malleus Maleficarum,*' my uncle B confesses.

'What's that?'

'Another book. Not written yet.'

'Do we write it? That one too?'

'Of course.'

'I write *all* the books,' says my father the devil gloomily, grandly, watching the tear turn into a sore.

'Not without help from us,' says uncle B. 'The *Malleus*, for instance, is mostly our work. Astarot and me.'

'Under our own names?' the count says incredulously, stirring his drink with his tail.

'Of course not. Pen names as always. Krämer and Sprenger.'

'Sounds like a firm,' says uncle A.

'Dominicans,' says uncle B.

'Great.' My uncle Astarot sips his mescal with some pretence at daintiness, savouring the identity of authorship. 'When does it come out?' he asks, after a while.

'1486,' says uncle Beelzebub.

My uncle Astarot, who suffers from history as well as halitosis, loses interest. 'Another bit I enjoyed,' he said, 'was our Miss Venus here making sure that the goldsmith's little daughter was still a virgin.'

My father is hiding his painted face behind his hand. 'I did my duty,' he murmurs.

'You make a lovely nun,' says uncle A.

My father says sternly: 'As a matter of fact, it is really a question of *control*. We cannot afford my father in on things. That is why I made sure the girl would go straight to the convent of the Flaming Heart.'

'You didn't doubt Lucifuge Rofocale?' says uncle B.

'Lucifuge Rofocale is an authority on virgins,' says my father.

'Aren't we all?' My uncle Astarot is pouring another finger of mescal. 'Author, authorship, authority,' he says. 'I like it. The world is our book.'

My father licks his black lips. His tongue is like a phallus.

24

Wait. Let's get this straight.

Just hold it there.

My father, in drag, made some kind of love to my mother, while my uncle was watching disguised in the skin of a monk.

I see.

Go on.

25

My father the emperor Lucifer licks his black lips. His tongue is like a phallus. 'Dreams,' he repeats, 'I do not like. In dreams begin responsibilities.'

'So what went wrong?' says uncle Astarot.

'The friar fell asleep.'

'But why,' says my uncle Astarot, picking his teeth, 'did the friar fall asleep? And *how* did he fall asleep?'

'I fear,' my uncle Beelzebub says again, 'that his falling asleep was my fault.'

'It wasn't in the plot,' says uncle A, looking.

'My concentration,' uncle B explains. 'It wavered for a moment.'

My daddy writhes. 'You were lusting after the girl.'

'Get him going on about the cocks in the sewing box . . .' says uncle A. 'The dirty old sow. I loved that bit.' He sucks the mescal up the side of his goblet. 'Listen,' he says, 'did I ever tell you the story of Sir Gawain and the Sleeve Job?'

'I am God's eye,' my father says, descending from his pot, 'and I go to and fro in the earth and I walk up and down in it.'

Count Astarot has to wipe his master's arse on the pallium.

'. . . Alleluia!' says my father.

'What?'

'That hurts!'

'Perfectly good pallium,' says my uncle A.

'Oblates of Saint Frances of Rome?'

'Yup.'

'Two lambs?'

'Yup.'

'Blessed in the church of Saint Agnes on her feast?'

'Natch.'

My father winces. 'Well, the Pope's mind must have been on something else when he blessed it.'

'About the Sleeve Job . . .'

'Never mind the Sleeve Job,' says my father. 'That will do. I am wiped.' His third eye burns as he watches my uncle Beelzebub picking the membranous wings from the meso-thorax of a blue-bottle. 'You were *lusting* after the girl,' he says once more.

'She looked appealing,' the prince confesses. 'It was the way she said *hope*.'

'Hope?'

'The way in which her lips came together on the P.'

My uncle Astarot is examining his toothpick. 'I should have thought,' he says, 'that it would be difficult to say hope *without* bringing your lips together on the P.'

'I refer to the sweetness of it,' says Prince Beelzebub, 'not the mere incidence.'

My father the emperor Lucifer is drawing himself up to his full height. Thus, he is quite long.

'Free will is going to come into this now,' he says.

Uncle A moans and reaches for more mescal. 'I hate free will,' he says. 'I have never understood about free will. Not a word.' He turns on the prince. 'Letting the old pisser fall asleep! What were you thinking of?'

'I have told you several times.'

'The cunt in the case!'

My father says: 'There are techniques for coping with lapses like that. To tell you the truth, I found myself in a similar predicament just before she took her clothes off.'

'You mean you were excited?' my uncle A asks disbelievingly.

'On the contrary,' says my father. 'It put me out, that is all. The prospect turned my stomach, as did the knowledge of the pre-natal examination required of me consequent to such disrobing. In the circumstances, I fixed my mind on a letter of the alphabet.'

'I remember, I remember. R. For arse.'

My daddy raises his blasting rod.

'A million pardons,' begs the count, cowering exaggeratedly before the golden pot. 'Hey,' he adds, trying to change the subject, 'Maybe the Pope's economizing. One lamb? Half a fleece? Now Sir Gawain – '

My uncle Beelzebub is saying:

'I wouldn't criticize you for the rosemary or the roebuck, cosmocrator. But I was less impressed by your anti-feminist outburst while the abbess was shaving the girl.'

'Put it down to the closeness of my relation to an all-male family of three.'

'Even allowing for your relations,' my uncle Beelzebub says, 'it struck me as too much in your own voice and not enough in the nun's. There are rules for such things.'

My father giggles. 'And I make them.'

'So you can break them too?'

'Sod's Law,' the devil says.

'I liked the frigging best,' says uncle A with relish. 'The frigging was bloody fine. Especially when you made her wriggle about on that stone floor with the candle.'

My father shrugs his heron's shoulders. 'Not difficult,' he says. 'Nuns do.'

'Oh flypaper!' says my uncle B. 'Nuns don't.'

'You mean that no nun ever stuck a candle up her nasty female orifice?' demands my father. 'You are seriously claiming that there was never a nun who masturbated herself with a candle?'

'Of course I am not claiming that,' says my uncle Beelzebub. 'What I am pointing out is the excessiveness. You went too far. You made her do too much. You had her behaving at the end there almost like a parody of celibate sexuality gone mad.'

My uncle Astarot is winking at the emperor. 'Amen,' he says. 'Listen to the professor, lord of the gnats, god of the midges. And who tossed himself off down a hole in a ceiling?'

'A friar called Blaise,' says uncle B lamely.

'And who was possessing him at the time?'

Prince Beelzebub's sigh is half resignation, half regret. It hangs like a bright exhalation on the evening.

'Friar Blaise has palms made for the cupping of his own seed,' he says. 'Pearlpale grails. His nature is not chaste. Besides, the law of demonic possession is only that the possessor does not compel the possessed to do anything absolutely counter to his body's or his soul's reason.'

'Or to the unreason that underlies their union,' the devil reminds him.

'An important point, yes,' Beelzebub concedes, buzzing. 'But then the opposite, in terms of behaviour, is always implicit in the psyche. It is no great magic to turn a man into his shadow.'

My uncle Astarot is finishing off the bottle of mescal.

'Which one wanked then?' he demands. 'The friar or the friar's shadow?'

'No doubt they were both moved in the circumstances,' says my uncle B mildly.

The three devils look at each other.

Little pig, an abomination of desolation.

My father is fluttering his hands.

'Listen,' he says. 'Listen to the worm.'

It is certainly making an unusual noise.

'The last time it sang like that,' the devil says with a happy leer, 'was just before the Anomalous Woman went and dropped my brother in the cow shit.'

26

I have been studying my crystal cave. It seems to me to be made of clear transparent quartz, rock crystal, probably formed from water by the exercise of intense cold. Here I am, a man shut in a frozen raindrop.

27

Friar Blaise dreamt of a tower of bronze.

Now he has made his dream come true.

A tower of bronze on Mons Badonicus, my Jesus.

My mother the virgin Vivien is bewildered by the one-eyed friar.

His mind changes so often, brother wolf.

It is you might say a wonder that the tower was achieved, for one day Friar Blaise would build and the next day he would burn.

All the same, in the end, and almost as it seems despite himself, or contrary to the dictates of his conscious will, the tower is completed.

My mother lives in it.

The door is kept locked.

My mother is attended by the abbess of the convent of the Flaming Heart and by another nun, a Sister Mary Contradiction.

The nuns are kind.

Sister Mary Contradiction is a bit of a mystery. She doesn't say much, my Christ. Her character seems colourless and transparent, making it fatally easy to imagine her and to imagine that one understands that imagination. She obeys her abbess without demur. Nevertheless, Dame Pudicity does not seem to like her. At the same time, something seems to prevent the abbess from sending the older woman packing.

The tower is tall and strong.

It affords good views over the parks and marshes.

From its topmost turrets, on a clear day, you can even sense in the farthest distance the green beginnings of the forest of Broceliande.

Friar Blaise calls the tower Anthanor.

As my mother's time draws nearer, Dame Pudicity is most solicitous and attentive. When Vivien fancies Jericho dates, for example, the nun comes back with a basket of them on her arm. It is the same with sweet pickles and honey-figs soaked in Cyprus wine.

'Miraculous!'

'Not at all,' says the abbess. 'These little things just drop into your lap when you have reached my place in this world.'

The pickles in particular are delicious.

Dame Pudicity's behaviour is sometimes odd, but never again as bizarre as it was on the night of my mother's examination at the convent.

My mother is glad of this. Since she felt me kick in her womb, she has become concerned about my life as something quite distinct. She does not want me harmed, or growing up to be some kind of freak.

The virgin Vivien sees Sister Mary Contradiction as a motherly body, animated, amiable, dressed in blue velvet, as bright as a hazel stick. To the young girl's eyes, there is an air of romance about her. Drifting hither and thither about the tower of bronze, locking and unlocking its thirty padlocks, invariably carrying a miniature blue bottle of salt water tied to her cincture, sitting and staring at the knife plunged into the meat or the windy spiral staircase leading down to the only door, the funny little nun imparts to the most trivial things that she says or does a certain charm which one so rarely finds in them.

When evening comes, she is easily and often persuaded to sing a canticle in honour of Vivien's unborn baby. She does not forget to extol Vivien herself for her goodness and her simplicity. Sister Mary Contradiction's heart seems infinitely sensible, unswayably the same, and always absorbed in the beloved object.

On Christmas Eve the child is born.

Me.

28

'*Jesus Christ!*' says the devil my father, and all hell breaks loose.

29

It is in the very instant of my father the emperor Lucifer saying *Jesus Christ* that Sister Mary Contradiction swings her cincture, smashing her blue bottle against the wall of the tower of bronze and splashing salt water over my emergent head, shouting:

'I baptize thee in the name of the Father and of the Son and of the Holy Ghost!'

Friar Blaise's sewn-up eye bursts open. Three Australian robber-flies buzz out. 'It's her!' he roars. 'It's the Anomalous Woman!'

'Eheia!' shrieks the abbess of the convent of the Flaming Heart.

And so shrieking she falls down on the floor of the tower of bronze and begins to writhe.

'Jod!' she snarls. And

'Tetgragrammaton Elohim!' she squeals. And

'El!' squalls. And

'Elohim Gibor!' she screams. And

'Eloha!' she screaks. And

'Adonai Sabaoth!' she shrills. And

'Elohim Sabaoth!' she squeaks. And

'Sadai!' she screeches. And

'Adonai Melech!' she shouts. And then

'Fuck the whole lot of Him!' she adds.

Now, as my mother the virgin Vivien watches, strange unexpected things come out of Dame Pudicity's mouth in the wake of these words.

What things?

A deep green *achmardi.*

Acorns.

Albes.

Ants.

Aurochs.

Beeswax.

Belladonna.

Bog myrtle.

Candlesticks.

Carbuncles.

White carnelian.

Caryatids.

Charcoal.

Chessmen.

Cockles.

A crown of thorns.

Two cuttlefish.

A deluge of diamonds.

Figs.

Frogs.

A gold crest wren.
Grapes.
Hailstones.
Hellebore.
Hemlock.
Seven homunculi.
An ipsissimus.
The Laidley worm.
A lingam.
A plague of locusts.
Lugworms.
Mercury.
Mice.
Murex.
Myrrh.
Nightingales.
Nuts.
Olives.
An onion.
A quail.
A quince.
A rook.
A rose.

The abbess of the convent of the Flaming Heart draws breath. Then more things issue forth from her mouth.

Namely:
Salt.
Sapphires.
Sards.
Sardines.
A scorpion.
The Ten Commandments.
A thurible.
Several vipers.
A quantity of vitriol.
A great number of weasels.
A cracked world egg.
The roots of the tree Ygdrasill.

The two Australian robber-flies have been buzzing rather dislikeably about my new-born head. Their bodies are $1\frac{3}{4}$ inches long, with a wing span of $3\frac{1}{4}$ inches.

Friar Blaise succeeds in opening the wound of his empty eye-socket and the flies return whence they came.

The monk has been looking on helplessly at Dame Pudicity's production of vomit. Now that she has finished, he turns aside and remarks to my mother:

'The abbess is not herself today.'

My mother shrugs.

Sister Mary Contradiction cuts the birth cord with a shell.

My mother cradles me to her bare breasts.

'It's a boy,' she notices.

30

Friar Blaise is twisting the midwife's arm.

'Who are you?' he hisses.

'You know me,' that worthy answers. 'Mary Contradiction.'

'What kind of a name is that?'

The midwife belches. She gives off a smell of gin and bad eggs. 'Surely you understand the principle of contradiction, father? That it is impossible for a thing to be and not to be at the same time and under the same species.'

Smoke is trickling from Friar Blaise's eye-socket, where he pinches the flesh together to mend it, with the flies inside.

He says:

'And that is where you get your stupid name from?'

'No,' says the midwife sweetly. 'My name is in honour of a mystery. The mystery of free will, father. For what is essential to free will? Why the liberty of *contradiction*.'

'Freedom to sin?'

'Not at all. The freedom to sin is an abuse of free will, and so not of its perfection but of its imperfection. The liberty of contradiction is our freedom to do or not to do. Just that. And I am Mary Contradiction.'

Having delivered this speech, which employs a form of

syntax quite unlike anything she has ever employed before in anything she has said in the bronze tower, the midwife adds: 'And will you please stop twisting my arm? It is too late now.'

Friar Blaise takes a step back from her.

He puts up his hand to touch the hand already mending his eye-socket. Both hands are quickly blackened by the smoke now pouring from that enraged hole.

'Not too late,' he says desperately. 'Never.'

'Never is a short word,' answers Mary Contradiction. 'I do not think that I believe in never.'

She is patting my mother on the shoulder.

'Are you all right, dear?'

'Fine, thanks,' my mother says. 'And it was ever so kind of you to go and baptize my baby the minute his head popped out, but couldn't we have waited for the friar here to do it?'

Sister Mary Contradiction smiles. Her smile is more expressionless than her usual expressionless expression. 'I think we might have waited a long time for that,' she says. 'An eternity, perhaps.'

'I see,' says my mother.

She doesn't.

'But will it count?' she goes on. 'Your baptizing the child, I mean.'

'Our virgin mother has a point there,' sneers the friar.

Mary Contradiction shakes her head. 'No point at all, father, and you know it. Any person may baptize validly. Man or woman. Lay or religious. All that is required is water and the requisite words.'

'In an emergency,' the friar says.

The midwife points to Dame Pudicity lying in the puddle on the floor. 'If that doesn't suggest an emergency . . .'

'That came after the act of baptism,' Friar Blaise observes.

'Naturally,' says Mary Contradiction.

'So where was the emergency in the first place?'

'Here on earth,' says Mary Contradiction. 'And in heaven and in hell.'

'Big words,' the friar snarls.

His eye has stopped smoking.

Now, unaccountably, it starts to weep.

There *is* no eye, only the black raw wound across the empty socket, but tears are running down from it across his cheek and chin. The monk slaps and flicks at the tears with his fingers. He goes crimson with embarrassment. 'Excuse me,' he says abruptly. 'I do not understand this.'

His one good blue eye does not weep.

But tears keep welling from the smoky hole on the other side of his nose.

My mother is suckling me at her breast.

Much pleasure, Jesukin.

'It seems to me,' my mother says, 'that you're both talking perfect nonsense. Why, father, what's the matter? What *is* the matter?'

Friar Blaise does not answer.

Weeping from an eye that is not there, he stumbles to the window of the bronze tower, and jumps out of it.

31

'StiBeTTChePhMeFSHiSS!' says my father, which is a word the devil himself does not utter often, on account of its power (it is a line drawn on the Tree of Life, descending from 1 to 10 via the Pillar of Severity) and on account of its being difficult to pronounce if you have a tongue like an anchor. Nevertheless –

'StiBeTTChePhMeFSHiSS!' he says again, emphatically. And then: 'Don't just *hang* there! *Do* something!'

My uncle Beelzebub yawns.

'What do you suggest?' he says.

'What do I suggest? I suggest you *hurl* yourself headlong flaming from th' ethereal sky with hideous ruin and combustion *down* to bottomless perdition. I suggest you shine like a meteor streaming to the wind. I suggest you *fall*, my dear. Fall after him – and *fast*! I suggest from morn to noon you fall, from noon to dewy eve, a summer's day . . .'

'It's Christmas Eve,' the prince reminds his master nastily. He sits down on the seat of desolation. 'You get poetical when you're angry,' he observes. 'Look,' he adds, 'I don't like these falls out of high windows. You're the faller, not me.'

'Are you an angel or a flaming daddy-long-legs?' demands my father. 'A drop from a mere tower inflicts no damage on a prince of hell.'

Vaunting aloud, he still looks racked with deep despair, my dad.

'Face it,' advises uncle B. 'We've failed.' He crosses his ginger boots, one over the other, and studies the dark designs under his fingernails. 'Farewell happy fields,' he says. 'And so forth.' He holds up his red right hand and looks at it with distaste. 'Birth is nasty,' he declares, 'suicide is vulgar, and accidents even more so.'

Friar Blaise, complete with two Australian robber-flies in his cerebrum, is continuing to fall, head downwards, at a rate of thirty-two feet per sec squared. His brown robes are tumbled down around his ears. He looks like a dropped parcel with forked white hairy legs.

Overhead the moon sits arbitress.

'I must, however, apologize,' my uncle Beelzebub proceeds calmly. 'My concentration is all to pot again. First I got distinctly uncomfortable having to chat up the Anomalous Woman. Then I was momentarily undone by an awareness that the ever so Vivien was going to give her breast to her untimely offspring.'

My father says:

'You have a lot to answer for, ducky, and that's a fact. If you hadn't started lusting after her in that confession box in chapter 22 then most likely she wouldn't have come on so strong with all those invocations of my brother's Mama, and then their lot –'

'The will and high permission of all-ruling heaven,' my uncle B says wearily. 'He knew. She knew. They know the number of hairs on your balls, if you will forgive the expression.'

'Not so,' says my father. 'The mind is its own place.'

His third eye suffers a dim eclipse.

'Providence,' drawls my uncle Beelzebub, tickling his fingers in the silver brocade on his doublet. 'Foreknowledge.'

'Will! The unconquerable will!'

'Fate, my cosmocrator,' sighs uncle B. He smiles and smiles. 'Fixed fate,' he says sadly. 'Free will. Foreknowledge absolute.'

My father is giggling.

My father is writhing confusedly.

My father is clasping his head in his hands.

'Better to reign in hell,' he says, 'than serve in heaven.' And then, after an idle moment spent fiddling with his own nipples: 'Will you kindly shut up about my balls being hairy?' he adds. 'You know perfectly well that my balls are not hairy. You made that monk go on about my hairy balls – which he wants to imagine just because *he* has hairy balls and needs to identify with me – and here you are again claiming that heaven knows the number of hairs on my balls when heaven knows no such thing because there *are* no hairs on my balls at all.'

'So heaven knows that.'

'What?'

'That the devil's balls are bald.'

With grave aspect Lucifer rises. His form has not yet lost at all her original brightness. 'Look,' he said, 'what we should be considering is the question: *What happens next?*'

'God knows,' says my uncle Beelzebub.

'As you wish,' says my father. 'But He is not writing this book.'

32

Take no notice of their blasphemies, little pig.

It is my father's pride to imagine that *he* is writing this book with the aid of his lieutenants.

He was implying it in chapter 23. In a minute he will start asserting it openly.

That is always the case at this point in the story.

O Jesus, the cunning of the devil!

33

Uncle Beelzebub says: 'Me miserable!'

'*You* miserable?' says my father. 'What about me?'

'Which way I fly is hell,' says uncle B. 'Either re-assert myself, regain possession of this religious body, and avert the certain death that it will meet in seventeen thousand six-teenths of a second on the rocks down there. Or I let the idiot go, with all his trumpery.'

'We need him!' howls Lucifer.

'That hypocrisy?'

'He is essential to the plot,' my father says.

34

Apple tree, little apple tree, my sweetness, my friend, my daughter, *we shall see.*

35

'He is a cowl,' says my uncle Beelzebub. 'He is a hood, he is a habit, he is relics, beads, indulgences, dispenses, pardons, bulls.'

'Our man!' howls Lucifer. 'The sport of winds!'

My uncle Beelzebub shrugs, but his eyes are dark with excessive bright. 'You're howling just to keep your spirits up,' he says. 'Should we not concede that this scenario has not worked out? That the experiment has gone wrong? Cut our losses? Write *Finis* on the baby's brow? There will no doubt be another virgin and another chance. And next time we'll know better, won't we?'

'*Another* virgin?' shrieks my father. 'Myself am hell!' He tilts back his long oval face and shakes pestilence and war from his horrid hair. '*Another* book like this one?' His three eyes fill with infinite wrath and infinite despair. 'When I consider that,' he hisses, 'the hell I suffer seems a heaven.'

'I see,' says uncle Beelzebub. 'But an Antichrist born on Christmas *Eve* is not a bull's eye, and you'd better admit it.'

'I blame Astarot,' snarls my dad. 'He got the astrology wrong.'

'Where is Astarot?' my uncle B asks.

'Execrable shape!'

'Never mind. It was an idle question. When will you learn what should be clear as day, my emperor? Not everything depends upon astrology, or even us. There is free will. There are these terrible meaningless accidents. And there is – most horrible of all – what they call human nature. The virgin Vivien sees a mouse, or dreams of gorgons, or consumes too much quince jelly – and goes and has her baby one day early. We cannot be responsible for everything.'

Prince Beelzebub wraps a wing around his chief to comfort him.

Lucifer slaps him away. 'I spurn all pleasure when I'm on the job.'

'Pleasure,' murmurs my uncle B, 'was seldom further from my mind.'

My father is abashed. 'I blame myself,' he snarls. 'To some extent. Indulging in that oath. Letting all hell break loose. Allowing my attention to waver just in that fatal instant as the child was born. I gave the baptizing bitch her chance.' He spits rocks, caves, lakes, fens, bogs, dens, and shades of death. My sentence is for open war!' he declares. He shakes his blasting rod. 'An Antichrist born a day wrong is bad enough. A *baptized* Antichrist born a day wrong is one wrong too much.'

'He is your son,' Beelzebub says.

'Uck,' says my father.

'Does it mean nothing to you?'

'Much disgust. Some embarrassment.'

The devil picks up a dead soul, three parts flame. He lights one of his black cigarettes with it. He smokes a little, blowing perfect circles.

'I wish I could blow imperfect circles.'

'If you could,' says uncle B, 'it would be different.'

'The world?'

'The book.'
'Fiction?'
My uncle Beelzebub smiles. 'The art of blowing imperfect circles perfectly.'
'I shall never master it,' my father says.

36

My uncle Beelzebub jerks a thumb in the downward direction of Friar Blaise. 'So? It is agreed, on balance, that I let this creature go?'
My father the devil blows a square.
'Look at that,' he boasts.
'It's a *perfect* square,' my uncle B points out.
'Shit,' says my father.

37

My father says:
'Our monk is about to break his neck?'
'Yes,' says my uncle Beelzebub.
'And crack his skull in seven places?'
'I cannot guarantee seven, but more or less.'
'And smash his vertebrae?'
'Without doubt.'
'And spill his life blood?'
'All over Mons Badonicus.'
'O dark, dark, dark, what is the fucking point of it?' my father the emperor Lucifer shrieks, throwing his cigarette at his lieutenant. 'What, what, *what* is the point of the entire Antichrist programme if you go and let this foolish lecherous ridiculous old one-eyed ecclesiastical trashbin *die*? He is no use to me dead. Alive, it is just possible . . .'
'Cosmocrator, you are an optimist,' my uncle B remarks with an equable grimace.
My father is fuming. Then he giggles.

'I say,' he says. 'I've just thought of an awfully good name for it.'

'The story?'

'The son.'

'Yes?' inquires uncle B, out of politeness.

'Shit,' says my father.

38

'You will never persuade that little girl to call her baby Shit,' says my uncle Beelzebub. 'I lay odds on it.'

My father scowls, the eyebrows meeting over his three eyes. 'Pity,' he says. 'A perfect name. It justifies the ways of God to man.'

Then:

'Wait a bit, wait a bit,' my father says. 'I could get her to call him Shit if I got her to use a word for shit which she didn't know was shit.'

'Only it sounds like a name,' says my uncle Beelzebub.

'*Merde,*' says my father.

'A good try,' uncle B agrees patiently. 'I am sure that she has no French. But on the other hand, being English, why should she give her child a French name?'

'Welsh,' says my father. 'The girl is Welsh as a matter of fact.'

'Is she? Well, the problem remains . . .'

'It doesn't,' says my father. 'It's solved. She will call him Myrddin!'

The lord of the flies smiles at his emperor's ingenuity. 'I see how you got to be top angel,' he says.

'Myrddin. *Merde*-in. In the shit!' my father cackles.

He stamps the air with delight at his own cleverness.

My uncle Beelzebub feeds on his own thoughts. 'Listen,' he says at last. 'I am bored. I don't want to go on with this at all, to tell you the truth. It would be most agreeable to allow the friar to smash to bits and let the rest of the book take what course it likes without him. But I enjoy a wager, as you know. I belong to nine gaming clubs. I'll strike a bet with you. If you can get the girl to call her baby Myrddin, or some other shit-derivative, I will agree to rescue him and to go on. At least for the time being. On the other hand – '

'Done!' cries my dad.

39

My mother swats the gnat which has been buzzing in her ear. Doing so, she slaps her own face.

With one red cheek, she says:

'Myrddin. That's a fine name. I'll call him Myrddin.'

My Jesus, I look up!

I glare at her from the tit!

I shake my head!

Dame Pudicity, palely loitering with bucket and brush but otherwise none the worse for her vomit, says not a word.

'It doesn't sound exactly Christian to me, dear,' is Sister Mary Contradiction's opinion.

'Myrddin,' my mother repeats decisively. 'Myrddin.'

I burst into tears.

I sob and throb.

I gnaw at her nipple.

'Hush, little Myrddin. Hush a bye, boy,' my mother is singing.

Myrddin . . . !

The murdered gnat dies buzzing it.

40

'Somehow I am not convinced,' my uncle Beelzebub says. 'Myrddin? That name does not ring true. I cannot quite believe in Myrddin.

My father roars. 'You know what you can do with your beliefs! Get saving that friar! I did it! I persuaded her! *And* I got squashed for my pains . . .'

'Ah,' says my uncle Beelzebub, 'the management of flies and other buzzers is an art in itself. More than nine billion transformations and *I* have never been swatted. You should not practise other devils' tricks, and that's the moral.'

'Fuck the moral,' says my father. 'Catch the friar.'

My uncle Astarot appears.

'My dear count,' says my uncle B. 'And where have you been for the last two seconds?'

'Up Guinevere's.'

'. . .?'

'Don't like childbirth, as you know,' my uncle Astarot explains, 'and there's this King Arthur – '

'Oh no there isn't!' screams my father. 'And quite likely there never will be, unless Beelzie catches the friar.'

'But they call him the once and future king.'

'Shit! Sot! Primus! *Once* is not *yet*! Save the friar!'

My uncle Beelzebub sighs.

He glances at Friar Blaise.

The monk's head is three inches from the rocks.

He has made an act of perfect contrition and is about to die in peace.

My uncle Beelzebub stretches out a lazy wing and prevents it.

A wing the colour of twilight, little pig.

'Thank you,' says my father.

Friar Blaise bounces seven times on his head and then falls in a brown heap in a patch of nettles. He leaps up instantly, as the nettles sting his bum.

'My soul has magnified the Lord,' my father says. 'And my spirit has rejoiced in God my saviour.'

'You *what*?'

'I just remembered,' says my father. 'That's where I heard her sing before. The girl with the ape.' He laughs like a clock running down. 'It was a nice tune too,' he moans.

The White Book

1

A spring has broken through the ground beside my Glass Castle. I can see it. I look through my own reflection in the glass walls and watch the water spurt and plume and fountain.

Yesterday a madman came wandering through the wood. He was tearing the heads off dandelions and eating them. He kept trying to stamp out the sunlight. He thought the sunlight was some kind of fire all over the ground, and he was trying to stamp it out. Long yellow slippers.

Then he saw me behind the glass. He stopped and stared and then he laughed. It was not a friendly laugh, but it was not unfriendly either. No doubt he was startled to see a man shut in a glass castle in a forest clearing.

He imitated the way my hands were spread on the glass inside as I looked out. He made those hands look like drowned starfish. I clasped my hands behind my back immediately, and began pacing up and down as though I had something important to remember.

The madman laughed some more and stooped and drank from the spring, and was cured of his madness. I know he was cured because when he looked up again he could not see me. He shook his head as if to clear it and then walked swiftly away through the trees without looking back.

Today the ground broke bubbling on this side of the wall. The fountain has come inside Glass Castle! I have drunk the spring water also. Great brimming handfuls of it. Cold and good water, tasting of pine needles.

This castle is in the forest of Broceliande for sure. I am imprisoned in glass in a castle in a forest, a forest with its great roots in the sea, and the light that falls down through these trees is an underwater light. The creatures move like fish beyond the glass walls that immure me: roe deer, squirrels, wolves, wild boar. Through the green shadows, down the leaf-strewn ways.

Green trees, green glass prison, wild wood, my encompassing forest of Broceliande which begins and ends where the night begins and ends.

The wood that is always growing.

The tower that is always falling, but never falls.

The tree that is always burning, and always green.

Raise the stone and you will find me, cleave the wood and there am I.

The once and future fool.

2

Look at me now, little pig. Here I am on the day after I was born.

Christmas Day . . .

Covered with hair!

Hair on my chest and hair on my back, hair on my arms and hair on my legs. My feet are furry. There are tufts of red hair like beards in both my arm-pits.

My face is the one exception to all this hair.

I have a face like a swan's egg.

A swan's egg covered with ancient writing.

The eyes in this face are old and clear and blue as the winter sky through which the moon climbs over Mons Badonicus.

My nose is a busted beak.

My mouth is remarkable also, being like two gold leaves folded over, the one on top of the other.

My mother the virgin Vivien did not notice these characteristics on the day I was born. O little Jesus, some of them were not there. The hairiness, in particular, came overnight. On Christmas Eve I fell asleep on my mother's breast worn out with crying after she named me Myrddin. On Christmas Day I woke up covered with hair.

Gazing down at me, my mother starts to sing.

The sun is streaming into the bronze tower across valleys filled with snow.

My mother's song is a carol:

Then up spake Mary,
So meek and so mild:
Oh, gather me cherries Joseph
For I am with child.

Then up spake Joseph
With his words so unkind;
Let them gather cherries
That brought thee with child.

Then up spake the little child
In his mother's womb:
Bow down you sweet cherry tree,
And give my mother some.

Then the top spray of the cherry tree
Bowed down to her knee;
And now you see Joseph
There are cherries for me.

When the song is finished, I speak.

'Not Myrddin,' I say.

My mother crosses herself.

'Merlin,' I say.

'Myrddin?' says my mother.

'Merlin!' I say.

My mother says nothing. Dame Pudicity comes in, followed by Sister Mary Contradiction.

'*Merlin!*' I shout.

'Merlin,' says my mother, very frightened.

'Not Myrddin,' I say.

'No,' says my mother.

'Merlin,' I say.

'Merlin,' my mother repeats obediently.

I blow a kiss to Sister Mary Contradiction. 'I liked your song about her,' I tell my mother.

'. . .?'

I open my mouth to explain.

Sister Mary Contradiction disappears down the windy stairs.

I shut my mouth.
I turn my head and look at Dame Pudicity.
Dame Pudicity looks back at me.
Her face goes blank with horror as my mouth slowly opens.
She shrieks.
She picks up her white silk robe between her legs.
'*A rivederci!*' she cries.
(Don't forget, old wolf my friend, this person studied in Rome as a young nun.)
Now she flees from the bronze tower.

3

Good-bye, Mary Contradiction. Farewell, abbess of the convent of the Flaming Heart.

That is the end of the part played by these two ladies in my story. I heard a rumour years later that the pair of them had cropped up together in a circus at Byzantium. It is not essential to salvation to believe this.

A rivederci, papa.

4

I address my young mother from the tit.

'We can manage without the ugly sisters,' I say. 'But get the one-eyed friar to come and re-christen me.'

Friar Blaise has been acting more oddly than ever since his fall from the top of the tower. Summoned now by my mother to her bedside, he laughs when he sees how hairy I have grown.

'Never mind that,' says my mother. 'I'd be ever so grateful if you'd baptize him again though. He says his name is Merlin.'

That one eye glares at me.

'Baptism is once and once only,' says Friar Blaise. 'The child's name is Myrddin.'

I open my mouth.

The milk runs down my chin.

'Fly away, Beelzebub,' I cry.

Friar Blaise changes colour. From dry white to bright blue. He smiles and smiles.

'My daddy's little jokes do not amuse me,' I tell him. 'You take water and chrissom shell and name me Merlin the next minute, or it will be the worse for you *for ever*.'

Friar Blaise is considering the window again.

I stand up on my mother's belly.

I shake my little hairy fists with rage.

'Merlin!' I cry. 'You call me Merlin, or – '

My right hand opens to snatch at and catch the big blue fly which is buzzing from Friar Blaise's mouth –

'Or you die, my lord fly!'

Friar Blaise nods weakly, as though a nerve has been snapped in his neck.

He fetches holy water and baptizes me:

'I name thee Merlin.'

Afterwards, he crawls off.

I sleep content on my mother's breast.

My fist is still clutched tight around the fly.

In the middle of the night, I wake.

I touch my chest with my left hand.

I touch my legs.

My feet.

My arms.

Only when I am satisfied that all the hair is gone which had covered me like fur, do I unclench the fingers of my right hand and let my uncle Beelzebub buzz off.

5

'What are you?' my mother whispers fearfully as I lie in her arms.

I tell her the truth.

'I am a baptized Antichrist, half man, half devil.'

She does not understand.

She loves me.

She rocks me asleep in her arms as the snow falls from a noon sky the colour of night, snow filling the valleys and combes of England, making all the land a snow-filled Grail.

6

According to the law of that time, my mother has two choices. A woman who conceives a child out of wedlock may either

(1) Become a regular whore;

or

(2) Die.

Neither of these alternatives appeals to her.

The day of her trial approaches fast.

Bats swoop about the tower. My mother is afraid. One night she looks from the window and sees Friar Blaise going head-first down the ivy like a bat himself.

My mother weeps. I comfort her. I strut up and down the room in the top of the bronze tower, and sing songs, and tell her stories. I seem to have been born with stories in me. Now I unroll them and unfurl them for my mother's pleasing.

At Easter my mother the virgin Vivien is brought before the judge. I am with her. Friar Blaise accompanies us, his hands folded in his long brown habit, shoulders hunched, head bowed, the very image of a kite.

O Jesukin, your court is cruel.

My mother, examined, persists in the first declaration: 'I do not know the father of my child.'

'With whom have you had intercourse?'

'With no man.'

And so on. The judge refusing to believe her.

At last I can stand it no longer. I cry out:

'The devil take you, you false judge! I know my father better than you know yours!'

The judge places his chin upon the hilt of his sword of justice, and considers me. His moustaches hang heavy and low on either side of his face, and his long teeth shine like the ivory tusks of an elephant.

'What's this?' he says slowly. 'Witchcraft?'

'Fetch your mother,' I reply.

'I know,' says the judge triumphantly, 'it's ventriloquism, isn't it?'

'It is not ventriloquism. Fetch your mother.'

'What for?'

'Burning.'

'Burning?'

'I believe that is the penalty for bearing a child out of wedlock.'

The judge blinks at me. He wears a robe of vivid pink and velvet silk that spreads about the step on which his chair is placed. His hands are very beautiful, and ornamented with a clutch of costly rings.

'This is very strange,' he says. 'I do not understand how one so small – '

'Never mind my size. Will you kindly fetch your mother?'

'My mother is irrelevant.'

'Never say that,' I advise him. 'Listen, you are a bastard, and I mean that most sincerely. Your mother's husband is not your father.'

The judge's feet, small and well shaped, encased in gold slippers, jerk out from beneath the hem of his gown. He catches hold of the ivory arms of his seat. The sword of justice clatters to the floor.

'You and me,' I say. 'We're in the same boat.'

The judge throws back his head.

'*Mother*!' he howls.

The mother of the judge appears. Her hair waves about her like a flag. She should have been planted in a castle. She walks with a wiggle. As she goes past Friar Blaise she winks at him.

'Now,' says the judge, rubbing his slippered feet against each other, 'a little order and some logic here. A modicum of reality. A touch more of the law and what is expected, if you please. Mother,' – he leans forward proprietorially and with confidence in his chair – 'Mother, who is my father?'

'Tiger,' says his mother, smirking, 'I hardly like to say.'

'What?' cries the judge. 'You mean your husband – the man I called my father – that it is not him at all?'

'I hardly like to say,' his mother says.

The judge puts on his black cap.

'Then I command you,' he thunders, rising. 'I command you to name him, woman! To name my father. Mother! The truth now!'

His mother giggles. 'You do look ducky in your little black death cap,' she says. 'Just like your dad. You've your dad's look really. You take after him far more than you ever took after me. Oh, come on, tiger! I wonder you can't pick him out for yourself. You've got his nose, his eye, his judging manners . . .'

The woman unleashes her finger from the fold of her dress.

She points. (Her fingernail is painted black.)

'That's him,' she says. 'Behold, the man!'

Everyone turns and stares at Friar Blaise.

7

'Before my time,' my uncle B says modestly.

8

'In that case,' says the judge, 'in that case . . .'

'Your mother must be burned,' I say.

'I know. I can't do it, Mamma . . .'

Two tears run down the judge's elongated lozenge of a face and splash into his vivid lap.

His mother gazes up at him defiantly.

'Pull yourself together, tiger,' she commands. 'Remember who you are and what I did.'

The judge wipes his eyes on his sleeve. Then he shields them with his hand. 'Hrmp, reverend sir, do you have anything to say on the subject?'

Friar Blaise smiles.

'Guilty,' he says.

Applause breaks out, my brother wolf.

The judge fends it off with his arm. Now he sits looking at the backs of his hands. He has a red mole on his right hand, just below the knuckle of his forefinger. A last desperate hope occurs to him. He holds up his hand significantly. Friar Blaise's single eye does not wink or blink. The friar holds up his own right hand, and compares red moles with his bastard.

'Daddy,' whimpers the judge.

'Case dismissed,' he adds, after the briefest moment's thought.

The papal nuncio, a long lean fellow, who has been leaning against the wall paring his fingernails, now leaps abruptly forward.

'On what grounds is the case against the female person Vivien dismissed?' he demands, in a thin high voice like a castrato corncrake's.

'On the grounds,' says the judge, 'that she was a virgin at the time of giving birth to her child; or alternatively that if she was not a virgin then it is in any case not a child, having a power of speech and reason far beyond a child's grasp; or alternatively that even if she was *not* a virgin and it *is* a child then the whole thing is a Saxon plot to discredit our legal system and confuse the registrar of births and marriages and deaths.'

The nuncio nibbles at his thumbnail.

'Rome,' he says, 'is not going to like this.'

'And on the alternative but not supplementary yet crucial grounds,' says the judge, 'that I am damned if I am going to burn my mother for the same offence.'

'Is it claimed that the child Merlin is a priest's bastard?' the nuncio says.

'He is not,' my mother says indignantly. 'The nearest I ever was to a priest was absolution.'

'Then where is the comparison?' demands the nuncio, nudging Friar Blaise as if to assure him that he will come to no harm whatever the outcome.

'The comparison,' the judge says, 'is the fire.'

The judge draws himself up in his ivory chair. He looks old and tired yet suddenly full of spirit. Defending his mother has given him a dignity in the last few minutes, or perhaps more truly it has permitted him to re-find and re-assert whatever dignity he once possessed.

'I am sick of burning women,' he announces. 'I have been sick of it for some time. You have to draw the line somewhere, and I draw it here and now. I am not going to burn my mother. And having not burned my mother, it follows in justice that I cannot condemn another for my mother's sin – namely, that of conceiving a child outside of holy wedlock.'

The judge rises. He produces a fishing rod from under his pink robe.

'I'm going fishing,' he says. 'Court adjourned.'

The judge heads for the door.

'You can burn the stake,' he tells the nuncio as he passes him.

9

My mother the virgin Vivien dies nine days later of food poisoning contracted after eating a tench.

The judge's mother is knocked down by a chariot on the outskirts of Carbonek, refused admittance when she crawls to the convent of the Flaming Heart for care, and dies in a ditch of her wounds. The chariot driver does not stop.

The judge hangs himself when he hears the news, choosing the same willow tree to hang himself that has been used by his mother's husband when his mother's husband learned the truth about his wife's infidelity and the true parentage of the judge.

Friar Blaise dies in mysterious circumstances two days after these events. The coroner says that the one-eyed priest has choked to death on a fly.

The papal nuncio sends a satisfactory report to Rome.

After much giggling and scowling, he adds a PS, addressed as much to himself as to the Pope:

But what do we do about Merlin?

10

Agreed, brothers mine. In *that* sense they *are* writing this book . . .

But consider.

In chapter 33 of the last book my father claimed that Friar Blaise was essential to the plot. Now, for reasons best known to himself, he has written the monk right out of his own life.

Apple tree, little apple tree, my sweetness, my friend, my daughter, I promised you that *we would see* and now *we have seen.*

For the record: I cannot stop them doing it.

I write down what they say and do.

I follow what happens as it happens.

I want to have it true.

I am a man locked in the present tense.

Shut in these happenings as they happen.

All, all is present to me.

In my green prison.

11

I have this gift of seeing past and future. From my father, the one. From my mother, the other.

But I cannot change the happenings.

I cannot change the future as I must not change the past.

The most I can do, the once and future fool, is to make it come true again in the present.

Yes, little pig, I know what is going to happen.

Up to a certain point, which is always soon enough reached . . .

12

I see the seneschal Vortigern now as I saw him in my boyhood. I was not there in Logres where he was. I was looking in a trout pool on Mons Badonicus.

I see as I saw the seneschal Vortigern trying to scratch his bum on a usurped throne.

The children in the streets of Logres play at dragging corpses up and down.

Snow is falling on the burnt altars and lying in smoky drifts down the porphyry stair of Saint Paul's church.

At a window overhanging the river a woman is screaming.

Not a face turns up, not a single face turns up from the oars of the golden galleys or the reins of the iron chariots rolling away from the city down Watling Street and across the bridge.

The Thames runs with blood.

I see the seneschal Vortigern rise.

'The trouble with kingship,' he says to his druid, 'is that you can't scratch your arse properly when it itches. Do you think I could have a hole cut in the seat of the throne? Then I could keep my dwarf under the seat, below the hole, inside the throne – and when my backside is itchy I could have the dwarf scratch it for me. It would be easily accomplished. I need only drill with my heels against the legs of the throne. Two taps for a little tickle. Four for a right good scratch. Fogo does the rest. What do you think?'

'I think,' the druid says, 'that a king's bum should not itch.'

'Ha, you dispute my right?'

The seneschal Vortigern is indignant. He is touchy on the subject of his right to the throne, as is natural in a usurper.

'Not at all,' the druid says smoothly. 'I mean that as you get used to sitting on the throne so your bum will learn not to itch. It is a property of thrones.'

'I shall hope that you know what you're talking about,' says Vortigern. 'Meanwhile, I still favour the idea of the little circular secret hole. And Fogo crouched beneath me in the dark. Ah Christ, what a relief . . .'

The druid says nothing. He is priding himself on having said *It is a property of thrones* when what he meant was *It is a property of kings.*

Remember King Constance, little pig. This false Vortigern was once his seneschal. Who ever would have dreamed the throne would one day have to accommodate the bum of Vortigern?

My sorrow, King Constance had three sons – Moyne, Aurelius Ambrosius, and Uther Pendragon. When Constance died, the eldest of these sons, Moyne, succeeded him. But Moyne was young and doomed, with his death painted on his cheek. When the barons made war against the new king, it was a simple matter for Vortigern to decline to lead the army out against them, so that Moyne was defeated. Then the barons asked Vortigern to take the crown. 'I am flattered,' he said, 'but it's something I couldn't do in all conscience while the young king lives.' The barons took their cue. Moyne was smothered in his sleep that night. Vortigern paid the murderers, when they came to ask for their reward, by having them torn apart by horses. O little Jesus, I see two great dray horses with a leg strapped to each, and sundry other parts of flesh once belonging to the one man. The horses thunder whinneying through the dew. An image of the distance between man and the rest of creation: those innocent grey horses running through the meadows, from village to village, and under the green leafy boughs with their torn-apart luggage of flesh.

'I think I may be getting piles,' the seneschal Vortigern says. 'It is an occupational hazard of kings,' agrees his druid.

Morgantius steps out from behind the white shields with a kind of devil-may-care, loose, aimless gait, the brim of his hat pulled brigandishly down across one ear. He has his hands in his pockets.

'King,' he says.

Vortigern is grateful. His sad eyes wander away to the live coals, then come back and search the messenger's face.

But find nothing.

'You'd better get a good horse under you,' Morgantius says. 'The owners of that chair are coming.'

The seneschal squawks like a duck being strangled. His finger works hard in his bum. 'Kingship!' he belches. 'For two pins I'd sell myself to a circus in Byzantium.' He licks his black lips. He winks owlishly in the smoke. He shakes his head, disturbing the old shabby hat that serves him for a crown, making its circlet of blessed lead images jangle around the greasy brim, while with his free hand he fingers the medal of the true cross of Saint Lo which dangles in his groin. '*Timor mortis,*' he growls. 'Shit.' He stares with fish's eyes at the stone walls dripping with water. 'To be king is just to inhabit the best dungeon,' he groans. All

Logres seems to be under the level of the river. The city is rat-ridden, its houses infested with toads.

'How far away?'

'A week.'

'How many?'

'Twenty thousand.'

'Aurelius Ambrosius?'

'And Uther with him.'

Vortigern stands and sways. He wears a linen shirt and drawers, and a woollen tunic fastened with a belt. On his broad flat feet are bands of stuffs, vermilion, madder, blue, crossed with one another, and covering his scraggy legs to the knees also. He casts an otter's pelt across his shoulders.

'A week means a month,' he mutters. 'But twenty thousand means enough, even if it is ten.'

He kicks at a rat as he walks the long room.

'I want mechanics!' he screams. 'Mechanics and masons and artificers! Build me a tower! In the furthest west! In Snowdon!'

'Isn't this a little premature?' murmurs his druid. 'We haven't lost yet. There are still battles against Aurelius Ambrosius and Uther Pendragon to go through.'

'I know my fate,' says Vortigern, with a stab at dignity. 'And so do you,' he hisses at the druid, under his breath. 'God blast it, man, you're the one who read the entrails, aren't you?'

The druid shifts from foot to foot.

'Forty days!' screams Vortigern. 'Let my tower be built in forty days from now. If not – if not – All you artificers will be dead anyway! I will see that the sons of Constance catch you, and if you don't die on their swords then I will feed you to the Saxons.'

The seneschal stops, purple in the face.

'Forty days!' he commands, holding up his sceptre in one hand and scratching his backside with the other. 'Forty days and forty nights!'

13

The druid discovers a suitable hill in Snowdon and has the masons lay in the foundations. Three levels of stone have been raised up above the ground by the third day. But on the night of the third day the walls crack open and the stones fall down.

The druid takes a deep breath and tries again. Again three levels of stone are in place by the evening of the third day's working. But that night, in the dark, the hill suffers a small earthquake and the stones fall down again.

The druid giggles. Then he lies down on the green hillside and writhes. He thinks among other things of Aurelius Ambrosius and Uther Pendragon, their hard blue eyes, and the north wind at their backs.

'One more try,' he tells the workmen.

The workmen hammer and carry. By the night of the third day there are three levels of stone wall in place once more.

Tonight the druid stays up in the moonlight watching the tower.

At half past two in the morning the ground shakes once.

At a quarter to three the ground shakes again and some dust comes down from the tower.

At three o'clock the whole hill is shaken by a violent earth tremor and the tower falls down completely.

The druid sits brooding among the fallen masonry.

With a long face, O Jesukin.

Dawn comes.

The druid lights a cigarette and smokes it, blowing at least three perfect smoke rings.

Then he rubs the side of his face with the ring on the little finger of his left hand.

The touch of the ring reminds him of something, and he giggles.

The druid has not been the papal nuncio for nothing.

14

The druid (who has not been the papal nuncio for nothing) cringes before Vortigern, with cock's blood on his fingers and exhaustion written all over his face as though he has been up all night at the chiromancy.

'Nothing can make the tower rise,' he says, 'but the blood of a fatherless child.'

'What kind of crap is this?' demands the seneschal. 'I kill a king and then a king. I want a tower. Where is it?'

A king and then a king is new to the druid, although of course he half-suspected it. He says nothing about this, however. Instead he says:

'The blood of a child born without a mortal father. That blood, smeared on the foundations of the tower, is the only thing that can avail to make it stand.'

'Say that again,' says Vortigern, scratching.

'Your tower will never be finished,' says the druid, 'unless its mortar is mixed with the blood of a fatherless child.'

'O yes,' says Vortigern, 'and where am I going to buy that?'

'Try Mons Badonicus,' says the druid.

15

After the death of my mother the virgin Vivien from the poisoned tench, there were seven attempts on my own life.

A beadsman tried to throttle me with a rosary.

A young nun tried to stab me with a sharpened crucifix.

A pilgrim tried to batter me to death with his staff.

A sexton tried to bury me alive.

A verger tried to hang me in some bell ropes.

Two choirboys tried to drown me in a font.

A bishop tried to brain me with his crook.

After this, I might have been forgiven, my brothers, if I supposed that there would be no more attempts on my life.

But I did not so suppose.

At the point now reached in my story, I am fifteen years old, and in the year of my fifteenth birthday the Romans have withdrawn from Britain. True, young men (though, more often, young women) are now at the mercy of marauding bands of Saxon pirates who come in from Germany and Denmark, across the wastes of the sea in their long ships with prows like beaks.

But Saxon pirates are not in the Pope's employ.

16

Apple tree, little apple tree, my sweetness, my friend, my daughter, I am playing in the street when the soldiers come. I see from their shields that they are Vortigern's men, and know from the trout pool what they want of me, and why, but I let myself be taken just the same.

Indeed, I draw attention to myself so that the soldiers know who I am. I do this by hitting the boy next to me. The boy hits me back. Whereupon I knock him down with a left hook to the side of the head.

(Brothers mine, delight in fisticuffs is natural to one who occupies his own body with disdain. I was born with a busted nose. That nose was broken again in a scrap when I was ten. It never set right, and its crookedness amused me whenever I looked in the mirror. It is good to be able to suffer a broken nose although you are a demigod. In my opinion, it is equally as good to be able to inflict them with skill. I am, at fifteen, a boxer, a wrestler, and a swordsman. It gives me pleasure, also, that my slight frame and gentle abstracted manner tend to belie such attainments and mislead my opponents before any altercation.)

The knocked-down boy gets up. 'Bugger off,' he says bravely. 'Why don't you just bugger off to nowhere, you fatherless freak?'

'Speak up,' I say.

'Everyone knows you're the devil's bastard,' the boy shouts. 'You fucking fatherless motherfucker you!'

At this, the soldiers take an interest in me. They seize me and put me in a cage, and haul me off to Vortigern in Logres.

The seneschal says: 'Your name is Merlin?'

'I am Merlin.'

'And you had no father?'

'My father was the devil.'

Vortigern shakes his head with a nervous smirk of superstition. 'Can such things be?' he asks his druid.

'According to Apuleius, yes,' says the druid, who is eating an onion, one of many which bob in a vinegar bath on his knees. 'In the *De deo Socratis* you will find him saying that between the earth and the moon there are spirits which he calls incubus demons. Their nature is partly that of men and partly that of angels. It has been known for these incubus demons to have intercourse with young women in the provinces.' The druid giggles, his mouth full of onion. He is quite black, save where a three days' beard lends a gleam of snow to his chaps and chin. Being toothless, he is an indifferent performer upon the onion. 'There was even a famous case at Sodom,' he says, 'where two of these incubus demons were required to have intercourse with young *men* . . .'

I consider the druid.

'Go down, Lucifer,' I say.

And then, with a touch of affection: 'Father?'

The druid writhes. He is a long queer fellow. 'There must be some mistake,' he says lamely. 'My name is Honorius.'

'Strange how you resemble a Pope's man I once knew.'

'I was a nuncio,' the druid admits, 'in the bad old days before religious freedom.'

'And even before that,' I say, 'weren't you once in the shape of a nun called Pudicity?'

The seneschal spits. 'I do not like to hear of such things,' he says. 'What you describe is quite ridiculous in any case. Honorius is a man. I have no sex-change freaks in my court.'

I muse aloud. 'Why was Friar Blaise killed by the fly? Internecine warfare between demons. Or did *his* devil get too much for him? So . . . So . . . My father killed my mother, and now for an eighth time he tries to kill me . . .'

'I thought they said you had no father?' says the seneschal. His bum is itching horribly. 'Well,' he goes on, 'there's one sure way to find out whether you *are* the fatherless brat we need. Bring me some mortar here. Fogo, cut his throat!'

Vortigern's dwarf leaps on to my shoulders.

He presses a knife to my windpipe.

Cackling, he starts to cut.

My hand comes up absent-mindedly, as if to bless myself for a last time.

I seize the dwarf by the hair.

I swing him in a circle round my head.

The dwarf is screaming.

Idly, I throw him against the wall.

Crack!

There goes his skull.

His blood spatters the seneschal.

'Listen,' I say, 'and I will tell you why you cannot build your tower.' I am speaking to Vortigern, but my eyes never leave Honorius. 'In the first place, it is because you are not fit to be king and your sins pursue you to the ends of the kingdom you usurped. In the second place, as I think your druid knows well, it is because your sins have taken specific root and shape *inside* the earth of the kingdom. For under the tower is a pool, and drain the pool and you'll find a great worm that swallows its own tail and sometimes fights against itself. When it divides it becomes two worms – a red worm and a white. No doubt it is fighting now. No doubt it is the alchemical war to the death between the red worm and the white worm which is causing the ground to shake and to break, and to throw down your tower again and again.'

'StiBeTTChePhMeFSHiSS!' screams the druid Honorius. He falls down on the paved stone floor and writhes. 'Bugger! Your! Being! Baptized!' he cries convulsively, as strange things bucket from his mouth. What strange things?

A deep green *achmardi*, acorns, alabes, ants, aurochs, beeswax, belladonna, bog myrtle, candlesticks, carbuncles, white carnelian, caryatids, charcoal, chessmen, cockles, a crown of thorns, two cuttlefish, a deluge of diamonds, figs, frogs, a gold crest wren, grapes, hailstones, hellebore, hemlock, seven homunculi, an ipsissimus, the Laidley worm, a lingam, a plague of locusts, lugworms, mercury, mice, murex, myrrh, nightingales, nuts, olives, an onion, a quail, a quince, a rook, a rose, salt, sapphires, sards, sardines, a scorpion, the Ten Commandments, a thurible, several vipers, a quantity of vitriol, a great number of weasels, a cracked world egg, the roots of the tree Ygdrasill.

When the druid has finished being sick, his body lies quite still.

His toes turn up.

He is dead.

Indeed, the druid seems more than dead – for his body lies like a cast-off glove, as though it has never had any life of its own.

The dwarf and the druid lie side by side on the stone paved floor.

The seneschal Vortigern stands gazing at them for a long while, sucking his teeth and scratching his arse.

Then he says:

'Dig under the tower for this pool. See if it's true, what he says.'

17

The seneschal's men dig.

It is as I said.

There is a great underground cavern, and in the cavern water.

They drain the pool and find two worms, one red, one white, each worm as big as a sea serpent, the two of them locked in a fight to the death. (The diggers think at first that it is one worm, red and white, so closely entwined the two creatures are.) Fire licks from their lips. They fight horribly.

Once the pool is drained, the war of the worms becomes madder. They throb and thresh like something supernatural in its death agony. Now the red worm is on top, and now the white. Blood comes spouting from the mouths of both, and they sweat great gouts of blood too. In the end the red worm hangs dead at the edge of the pool, while the white worm pours itself back into a dark and stinking hole that seems to run down into the bowels of the earth.

'What does this mean?' screams Vortigern.

My body falls down and dances in the dirt. When I return to it again I cry out in a prophesying voice:

'Death to the red worm! The Sleeve Job! Diana's manor! The brachet chasing the hart and the fifty black hounds chasing the brachet! Free will! YHVH! The lance of Longinus! Who the hell is writing this book? The male members in the sewing box! The sword in the stone! The nature of evil! The right question to ask the Holy Grail! My birth and deaths! King Arthur and the knights of the Round Table! Long live the white worm!'

'Enough of this squit,' says Vortigern.'What about *me*?'

'You,' I say. 'Find refuge if you can! But who may escape the shape of his own story?'

'What a load of verbal diarrhoea!' Vortigern sneers.

He whips his masons back to work on the tower.

Which goes up quickly enough now that the worms are gone.

'See?' says Vortigern. 'I shall be safe. I'm not intending to fight against these stupid sons of Constance. They can have the crown. I'll leave it for them on this oak. (Is it an oak? I've never been able to tell one tree from another. Who cares?) As for me, I'm going into my tower and I'm staying put, that's what. I've enough food and drink for a twenty year siege. I've swans to wipe my bum on. Fuck Ambrosius and that fucking Pendragon. Logres – they can keep it!'

The seneschal Vortigern goes into his tower.

Aurelius and Uther come.

When they find that they cannot take the tower by force, or winkle Vortigern out of it, they put straw and bales of hay all round about it, and surround the walls with hay wagons, and then set blazing brands to them.

The tower is soon like a great torch on the hilltop.

Vortigern climbs higher and higher inside, but the fire comes after him.

He is burned to death on the flagpole.

18

Aurelius Ambrosius turns his armies against the barons who supported Vortigern. He defeats them, and their Saxon allies also, at the battles of Maisbeli and Kaerconan. He cuts off the head of the Saxon chieftain, Hengist.

That head hangs on a hook when he summons me.

'You are a witch?'

'I am Merlin. Men call me a witch.'

'Because you can read the future?' Aurelius Ambrosius laughs. 'Tell me some marvels then. Astonish me. How will I die, for a start?'

I look into dead Hengist's staring eyes. I see Aurelius lying ill at Winchester, and a Saxon disguised as a monk mixing a poison which the sick king drains at a gulp.

'Mysteries cannot be summoned up for an entertainment,' I say.

Aurelius is disappointed.

I divert him with a different thought.

'What about a war memorial?' I say.

'A war memorial?'

'At Killaraus, in Ireland,' I say, 'there is a ring of stones called the Giants' Dance. The stones are enormous. If they could be placed here as they are there, round this plot of ground, they would stand for ever as a monument to your victory.'

Aurelius Ambrosius laughs again. 'And how do you propose to get them here? By clapping your hands and stamping your feet? As if Britain doesn't have big stones too! Why, we passed some down river there quite adequate for such a job!'

'Try not to laugh at what you do not understand,' I advise him. 'The stones of the Giants' Dance are no ordinary stones. They have healing virtues. If you wash the stones and put the sick in the water, the water will heal them. Mix the water with wine and it mends the wounds of battle too.'

Aurelius Ambrosius looks sceptical.

'Shall I fetch them?' I ask him.

'Go ahead.'

I sail to Ireland in company with the king's brother, Uther Pendragon, and fifteen thousand men. The winds are fair.

The Irish ride to meet us, under command of a king called Gillomanius. They fight fiercely, but I perceive a point in their flank which will give way to our sudden attack. We carry the day. The Irish flee.

(I have no military genius, little pig. Put it down to accident, or inspiration. Sometimes, thinking of one thing, you may achieve another. I was thinking of my mother at the time – how wretched her young death, how vile my father.)

When our fellows see the Giants' Dance they are filled with awe and wonder.

'Try your strength,' I tell the captains. 'See if brute force can move them!'

They rig up hawsers and ropes. They prop up scaling ladders. They sweat and pull.

Result: nothing.

The stones will not budge an inch. The Giants' Dance stays dancing in a still ring where it is.

'Stop fooling,' Uther Pendragon says shrewdly. 'Only Merlin can move these stones. Right?'

Right.

The Giants' Dance is removed that night, and placed in our ships, and carried to Britain, where I have the stones put up again in a circle just as they were on Mount Killaraus in Ireland.

This is now the monument called Stonehenge.

How did I do it?

ASTRACHIOS, ASACH, ASARCA, ABADUMABAL, SILAT, ABABOTAS, JESUBILIN, SCIOIN, DOMOL.

That's how.

And

ASTAROT ✠ ADOR ✠ CAMESO ✠ VALUERITUF ✠ MARESO

etc, etc, etc.

Leaving two exhausted uncles at the end of the day.

19

A comet comes out of the east and travels through the night sky. In its tail is the shape of a dragon. From the mouth of the dragon two rays of light issue – one stretching over Gaul, the other ending in seven smaller shafts that fall towards the Irish Sea.

Uther is marching west into Wales with the army when he sees the comet. He calls me before him to explain its significance.

'Your brother Ambrosius lies dying,' I tell him. 'He has been poisoned by a Saxon called Eopa, who has shaved off his beard and had his head tonsured, and come to the king in the guise of a monk. Eopa prepared a cup of death. At this moment he is instructing your brother to snuggle down under the bed clothes and go to sleep – the poison will work quicker that way.'

'Is there nothing we can do?'

'Nothing.'

'I will follow this Eopa to the ends of the earth,' says Uther Pendragon. 'I shall not rest until he has paid the penalty for his murder of my brother.'

'That may be more difficult than you think,' I say. 'I see him standing by the dying king. He grins like a fox eating shit out of a wire brush.'

'What does that mean?'

'Ask me nothing you can guess.' I change the subject quite deliberately. 'There is more in the picture drawn by the comet. In Wales now you will meet with the Irish king Gillomanius, who had joined with the Saxons to march on Logres. You will defeat them all in battle. Victory shall be yours, and Uther Pendragon will be king of all Britain! And your son, who will reign after you, will be greater yet!'

'All this in a scribble of stars?' says Uther.

'All this,' I say. 'Look at the sky. Ambrosius your brother is the comet that dies. You are the dragon. Your son is the light that spills from the dragon's mouth.'

Old wolf, this is my first prophecy of the coming of Arthur.

And the rest comes true, just as I said.

Uther defeats the Irish king in battle, and kills him.

He rides then towards Winchester, at the gallop. But it is, of course, too late. Messengers meet him on the road. They tell him that Aurelius is dead.

Uther has his brother buried with all kingly honours in the ring of the Giants' Dance. Remembering what I read in the sky, he also causes two dragons to be cut in gold, in the likeness of the dragon which I saw in the tail of the star. One of these dragons he gives to the city of Winchester, where Aurelius died on the day of the comet's appearance, and where it is kept in the cathedral. The second dragon he has made in such a fashion that it can be carried in front of his army, and from this day on Uther has the dragon precede him into all his battles.

20

Already I have enemies, O Jesukin. They talk about me in the corners of Uther's court, and behind closed doors. One of them, a baron called Cunedda, elects himself spokesman of the party.

'This Merlin is a charlatan,' he says. 'There's no such thing as witchcraft. It can all be explained quite rationally. The bringing of the stones from Ireland – elementary mechanics. The prophecies – confused poetic rantings. I don't accept a supernatural portion in any of it.'

I say nothing.

Determined to discredit me, Cunedda dresses himself as a merchant and comes before the court at Logres, asking how he will die.

'You will break your neck in falling from your horse,' I say.

Cunedda the merchant goes away. A week later he comes again before the court, this time disguised as a priest. 'Can the great white witch tell me how I shall die?'

'You will be hanged,' I say.

A third time, Cunedda presents himself at court. This time he wears the full panoply of a knight errant. 'I have come to discover from Merlin the magician how I shall die,' he says.

'You will drown,' I say.

Cunedda strips off his third disguise. 'Observe the contradictions,' he declares, exulting. 'Because I was differently dressed, this fraud has proclaimed for me three different and distinct deaths. How can anyone believe again a single word that he has to say?'

I eat an apple.

I say nothing.

I spit the pips as I listen to the music of the viol.

Leaving the court, Cunedda's horse stumbles. Cunedda falls. His neck breaks as he hits the ground. His head is entangled in his stirrups, however, and he is dragged for a mile by the runaway horse, being hanged in the process. At last the horse reaches the bridge over the Thames by the chapel of Saint John at Southwark. The horse plunges into the river, the stirrups snap, and the body of Cunedda is swept down river and out to sea on the ebb tide.

21

Here begin the terrors. Here begin the miracles.

I take Uther Pendragon into my confidence. I explain to him that I owe my knowledge of the past to my nature as a demon, but that such knowledge as I have of the future comes from God and is due to my mother's goodness.

'The devils have lost me,' I tell him. 'I will never do their will.'

Uther's own interest in heaven and hell is no more than flickering.

To strengthen his faith, I tell him the high history of the Holy Grail.

'It is the cup which was used at the Last Supper,' I say. 'It was brought secretly to these islands by Joseph of Arimathea. It was to be kept at Glastonbury, the Lake of Glass. But the cup was lost . . .'

'How?' demands Uther, a practical man.

I shake my head. 'Perhaps it was never found.'

'You mean it did not exist?'

'O the Grail exists,' I say. 'Be sure of that. It holds Christ's blood.'

'That is a great treasure,' says Uther, indifferently. 'You know, Merlin, I shouldn't be surprised if Euripides was right.'

'Euripides?'

'He wondered if life was death, and death was life. Maybe we are actually dead, you and me, and our bodies are our tombs.'

'That is another starting point,' I say. 'Given that we are dead, or imprisoned in ourselves, then the art lies in some work which will bring us to life, and free our spirits.'

But already I have lost the king's attention . . .

'You must know,' I say, 'that while the Grail cannot be achieved just by willing it, there is something else that goes with the Grail, and which it *is* within your power to achieve.'

'And what is that?'

'The table.'

'What table?'

'The third table.'

'I see. And perhaps you'll tell me about the other two?'

'The first,' I say, 'was the table of Jesus Christ, at which the apostles ate on several occasions. This was the table that sustained bodies and souls with food from heaven. And the Lamb without blemish that was sacrificed for our redemption established this table.'

'The Lamb? You mean Christ?'

'Of course.'

'Who only the other day you likened to a monkey.'

'An ape.'

'All right, then. A big monkey.'

'An ape. He appears differently to different eyes. Enough of that. The second table was in the likeness of the first and in remembrance of it. This was the table of the Holy Grail, established in the time of Joseph of Arimathea.'

'And what happened to that?' demands Uther.

'No doubt it is still available, in some senses.'

‘Meaning?’

‘Your task,’ I tell the king, ‘is the setting up of a third table. The Round Table.’

‘Round for the roundness of the world?’

‘And the condition of the planets, and of the elements in the firmament.’

‘I like it.’

‘These three tables,’ I tell Uther, ‘signify the three powers of the Trinity.’

His eyes go wandering off. He is bored again.

‘Set up the Round Table here in Logres,’ I urge him.

Uther pulls a face. ‘The third? To follow Christ and Joseph of Arimathea? Wouldn’t that be blasphemous? Or presumptuous?’

‘Leave the reckoning to me,’ I say.

Uther gnaws at a hangnail. ‘An advantage of it being *round*,’ he says, at last, ‘will be that no man will be able to sit higher or lower than any other man.’

The Round Table is made, to my directions.

Fifty knights sit at it, but one seat is left void.

The Siege Perilous.

22

And all the time this quarrel in my head . . . Not between good and evil merely, old wolf my friend. No. It was never quite as easy as that. To be sure, it seems sometimes to me that I have an angel and a devil in me, and that my life is spent while they strugle, with first the one and now the other in momentary total triumph. But that is true of most men. It cannot finally be true of me. For I am not a man.

Merlin the more than human.

23

Merlin the less than man.

That dialogue with Uther cost me dear. I must have been exhausted after it. To identify so completely with my mother, to be the mouthpiece of the triune God . . . Not so simple for one who was born to be the prince of Christ's enemies, until baptized otherwise.

This leads me to a curious episode, inexplicable otherwise.

The Round Table is established, and –

I disappear!

For seven years!

For seven years, they say, no one sees me at Logres. Knights come and go, in the service of King Uther Pendragon. The Saxons are kept at bay, more or less.

A story goes around that I am dead. I have been torn to pieces by a werewolf, or struck by lightning thrown at me by a rival enchanter. My enemies do not greatly mind which version they believe. One of these, a knight called Sir Alaric, craves a boon of the king.

'My heart's desire is to sit in the seat which has always been empty,' he says. 'What keeps us from using it? The rankest superstition! Merlin is dead. I am not afraid of the consequences.'

'Wait until Pentecost,' says Uther. 'If Merlin has not returned by then, you shall have your heart's desire.'

Pentecost comes.

I don't.

Sir Alaric sits down in the Siege Perilous.

The most extraordinary thing happens. One moment the fat knight is about to sit on the seat, the next moment he is sitting down upon it, and the next moment he is sinking down through it and disappearing inch by inch!

'Hey! Alaric! Come back!' call his friends. 'Your bum has gone! Your feet! Your arms to the elbows! Your body's going!'

Sir Alaric is like a drowning man. He is like a man caught in his own death in a whirlpool, unable to subtract or abstract himself from the downward suction of it.

Only when he has disappeared completely do his friends stop laughing. Then they walk round and round the chair, crossing themselves in fear and pinching each other.

I come in at the doorway. I wear, as per usual, a black hat and cloak, and I am not smiling.

'Very clever,' says King Uther. 'Very fine, very funny. Now bring back Sir Alaric.'

I take off my black hat. I bow.

'I am sorry,' I say, 'but that is more than I can do. Sir Alaric has gone for ever. The Siege Perilous is for the knight who shall achieve the Holy Grail, and for no other.'

Then there is argument and speculation among all the knights who are present, concerning which of them, if any, will be the one who will achieve the Holy Grail.

While the knights debate, Uther Pendragon takes me on one side.

'I have missed you, conjurer,' he says simply. 'Where have you been these seven years?'

'Seven years?' I say, completely puzzled. 'I just stepped outside for a piss!'

24

'It is his only weakness,' says my uncle Beelzebub. 'He has no sense of time.'

'Not his only weakness,' says my father. 'Oh no, not at all his *only* weakness. He's human like the rest of them, or nearly so. This imprecise sense of the passing of time is just the *first* flaw in his armour that we have found. There must be others.'

They sit by the gates of hell, my father and my uncles, watching the outcast angels who took no part in the revolution. These angels are neither in hell nor exactly out of it. They are condemned to running round and round in endless pursuit of a mad banner, wavering meaninglessly before them in the dirty air. As they run these angels are pursued by swarms of wasps and hornets. Wasp and hornet stings produce a constant flow of blood and putrescence, trickling down the legs of the running angels to feed the worms and maggots which coat the ground. The ecology of hell is perfect, little pig.

'What are we going to do about *him*?' demands my uncle Astarot, jerking a claw in the direction of Sir Alaric, who has just blundered his fat way through the gate and is looking round at the sights with eyes that can't believe them.

'Punish his external senses with fire,' my father says.

'But hell has been harrowed, Emp.'

'An over-rated bit of farming,' observes my father. 'It sorted out the men from the boys, you might say, nothing much more.'

'As I understand the situation,' says my uncle Beelzebub, 'hell has hardly been harrowed at all. What did the ape and the girl get away with? Just a handful of pre-Christian souls who didn't properly belong with us or in the other place.'

'Old Testament trash,' says my father, nodding.

Beelzebub winces as an angel swats a wasp. 'All the same,' he says, 'and I dislike having to mention this, but – have you noticed a slight diminution in our power?'

'Diminution?' says my daddy. '*I* am not diminished! Not in the least diminished! No!'

'All the same,' says my uncle B, thoughtfully. 'Once upon a time we only lost control of one of them if our attention wavered and the subject fell asleep. Now it seems a good deal harder. Look at Astarot getting killed three times like that.'

'I didn't enjoy it,' my uncle A confesses.

'Our power is the same,' my father says. 'No more, no less. We find ourselves pitted in essential places against a Trinity raising itself to the fourth power, that is all. Merlin.'

'Your son,' says uncle A accusingly.

'The Antichrist that went wrong,' says uncle B.

My father catches Sir Alaric on his blasting rod. 'Perhaps,' he whispers. 'But perhaps not.'

'What do you mean?'

'Wait and see,' the devil says. 'I've a feeling that Merlin doesn't take after his mother somewhere very important, that's all . . .'

25

I say it as I see it, little pig. I am in Spiral Castle, where the walls are winds. Before the door of this castle is a moving wheel. No one comes in or goes out save when the wheel is still. The wheel stops only at the touch of her hand.

This place is like a bee hive inside, a maze of tunnels.

I am a man shut in a maze of himself.

26

Confused? Confusing?

What about *for me*?

I see it as it happens.

I hear it too.

Total consciousness. The pain of that. Imagine!

To be aware of past and future equally.

To be aware of here and devils.

No wonder I have retired to my esplumoir.

I hang in a cage between one world and another.

27

But I am comfortable, dear darling daughter.

The shadows flicker on the glass. They are all there is, and I am trying to understand them.

Their sense is like the sense of sunlight reflected off water.

My story.

I am trying to tell you light reflected off water.

Don't grasp, don't snatch, don't worry if you cannot always follow me. I must lead you to dark places. Because my nature is dark and always will be, so must my book be dark in places.

Sweet apple tree, one night soon you must be witness to the marriage of heaven and hell.

28

'Feasts,' I tell King Uther Pendragon. 'Honour the Round Table with feasts at Christmas and Easter.'

The first feast falls at Christmas. All the king's knights are present, and the barons also, and with them their wives and their daughters and sisters and nieces. So many lovely ladies. There is music and dancing. And, leading the dance, Igrayne, the wife of the dark Duke of Cornwall.

I see Uther Pendragon's eyes wax smoky with desire as he watches her tread out the measure of the dance.

Igrayne is beautiful.

Sensuous.

Yet demure.

In a black gown, with a rose like a sweet red wound between her breasts.

Round firm breasts.

Glossy auburn hair flowing down her neck, setting off the whiteness of smooth skin.

Dancing, the Lady Igrayne gives every impression of an intensely erotic nature, of reserved or half-awakened lusts, of resources of libidinousness kept in check just below the surface of her gestures, which are all graceful and flowing, long, sinuous, sensuous.

Her fingers are agile and slender.

Her waist small.

Her legs long and shapely.

There are shadows in her sleek hair from the torchlight.

Her red mouth seldom smiles.

She has a hungry look, the Lady Igrayne. But I observe the king observing that she eats little at the feast. She touches her lips with a handful of white grapes, cooling their red, but she does not bite. Her hunger is not for meat or apples or wine.

King Uther Pendragon dances with the Lady Igrayne.

I see their hands touch lightly in the turns of the dance.

The tips of Igrayne's fingers must be cool to touch.

Once, on a turn, at the head of a column of dancers, as befits the king and his chosen partner, Uther touches the palm of her hand, thrusting his own hand roughly and suddenly into it. He looks astonished by the heat of her flesh there. But the eyes of the lovely Igrayne are cool and dark as underwater as the king gazes back at her over his shoulder in the movement of the dance carrying him away from her.

'She dances like a lapwing,' I say, when the king sits down again beside me at the Round Table. 'Like a lapwing running on tiptoe.'

I have observed the king's lust.

'There's something here I cannot understand,' Uther says. 'She seems both whore and virgin. Something hot about her, something lickerish. And yet the heat is *held*. Contained in a purity and stillness. A fragility. Something inviolable no matter what a man did to her.'

Uther Pendragon drinks deeply. The wine runs down his beard.

'I want her, Merlin,' he says.

29

The feasting lasts until the twelfth night after Christmas. King Uther Pendragon lavishes gifts on the Lady Igrayne. When the court goes hunting he rides beside her, catching the head of her horse when the horse treads on a snake and tries to bolt. Uther draws the glove on Igrayne's arm, and his body bends to hers, brushing it lightly, when the hawk stands on her sleeve. Igrayne's eyes burn, watching the hawk stoop and take the leveret from the hillside. Uther does not look at the hawk at all.

On Epiphany Eve the feasting is ended.

The barons ride away – Gorlois, Duke of Cornwall, and his wife, among them.

Uther Pendragon rages for a month.

I have never seen the king like this before. I think I never knew him till this moment. Brother wolf, it is impossible to know any man until you have met him in the grip of a dominating desire. When you know a man in the moment of his reaching for what he wants most in all the world – then you know him.

I, Merlin magician, ponder this as I walk by the pools of Logres, where the white fish circle in the twilit water.

What is it that *I* want most in all the world?

I cannot say.

Am I then as cold as the fish, inhabiting their other world of water?

What world do I inhabit?

(Devil voices in my head.)

Are my desires as those of other men? Or do the needs of devils burn in my veins?

The questions pour in my mind. Unanswered. As I pace.

It is the first time I have ever been confused.

I smile at my reflection in the twilit water, considering the irony of it. My confusion is not due to any passion of my own, but rather to my bewilderment in the face of another man's passion.

At Easter there is further feasting at Logres. Igrayne comes back, accompanied by her husband. The Duke Gorlois is a sullen man, black-bearded, black-cloaked, his usual garb rising in velvet quilted to his chin.

He carries a black whip.

I say:

'To keep his wife in order?'

And am immediately shaken by the effect my words have – first on Uther, then on myself.

For the king goes pale with desire as I speak the words in his ear, and I sense some fantasy picture flash across a secret chamber in his skull. Some scene in which the Lady Igrayne, the virgin whore, stripped of her gown, bares her white back to her husband's whip.

And I feel a stirring of excitement and desire, myself – not so much at the idea of Igrayne chastised (though that, I admit, is not without its fascination), more at the effect my chance-spoken words have seemed to have upon the king.

I am thrilled by my own power to create the erotic fantasy in Uther's head.

This is another form of witchcraft.

Another?

Perhaps not.

Perhaps it is the source of the magic I know already. For here is some root at the dark root of all – an erotic nerve below everything, a source for all manner of imaginations and enchantments.

What men *do* follows what they *dream.*

Dreams are not a substitute for reality.

The real world acts out the dream, or is its necessarily imperfect copy.

30

Easter is kept imperfectly at Logres.

King Uther Pendragon's religious enthusiasm has never been great, and with his passion for another man's wife it seems to have disappeared entirely.

There are vigils and services during holy week, the usual offices of the church. But through all of them the king moves in pursuit of the Lady Igrayne.

He follows her in procession. He kneels behind her in the chapel. He observes every movement she makes, and tries to anticipate all the movements she might make.

They dance again together in the torchlight on Easter Day.

But Igrayne is wary now.

She is not reluctant, but she is wary.

The intensity of the king's interest plainly worries her.

She must be thinking that her husband the duke will notice it sooner or later.

O Jesukin, he does.

Upon the gift of a golden cup.

Uther gives the cup to Igrayne after the great Mass of Easter. It is a cup encrusted with jewels and inscribed with the words: *Drink out of this for my love.*

Gorlois sees it.

He says nothing.

But his dark eyes are darker and more brooding as he strides from the chapel behind his wife. He taps at his black boots with his whip.

The king retires early from the dancing.

I follow him, myself unseen.

Uther waits in the long corridor, lurking at the turn of the stair.

Quick light footfalls.

It is Igrayne!

Like a lapwing running on tiptoe.

The king looms up before her, a shadow in the smoky light.

'Madam,' he says. 'I must.'

'My lord king?'

'Madam, I love you. I cannot sleep or speak or eat or fight or do anything else because of you. I will never love life again unless we lie together. Come to me tonight in my bedchamber. I promise you – '

Igrayne is half leaning forward towards him, half bending away as he snatches at her long hands.

The whispered importunacy of his promise proves too much.

She turns.

She twists her hands from his grasping hands.

She flees.

King Uther Pendragon goes and stands where Igrayne has stood.

He aches for her.

He goes back to the table of the feast.

The seats are empty.

There is the place where she sat.

The king sits there.

I watch from the shadows.

'Leave that,' he barks to the boys who are clearing the table. Uther takes up the silver plate that Igrayne has eaten from.

He touches his lips to the silver goblet she has sipped from.

He matches his mouth to the bread she has left half-nibbled.

He fingers the arms of the chair where her fingers have rested.

He sinks to the floor and buries his face in the seat.

I am embarrassed, little pig.

I am seeing something nobody should see.

I try to tiptoe from the hall ...

A dagger stops me!

A dagger whistling through the smoky air, thudding into the great oak beam behind me, pinning my black robe to it!

(Of course, I knew it was coming.

Even in his love-besotted state, the king is still the king.)

Uther Pendragon stands over me. He draws his quivering dagger from the wall.

'I must have her, Merlin,' he says. 'I must and I will.'

The fever of those blue eyes! The exact clear and burning colour of the alchemist's stone!

The king's eyes frighten me, O Jesukin.

Here is a power against which I am powerless.

Here is a fire I cannot comprehend.

Here in this woman is a witchcraft beyond my own.

'You hear me, Merlin?' Uther cries.

I draw the thread from my damaged sleeve. I wind it round my left thumb.

'There is nothing I can do about it,' I tell the king.

In the morning the Lady Igrayne is gone from Logres.

31

King Uther Pendragon rages like a beast.

He prowls.

He roars.

He ranges through the castle of Camelot in Logres, tearing at the arras, slamming all the doors, kicking and buffeting any servants who are stupid or unfortunate enough to get in his way.

'It's her husband!' he shouts. 'The duke has discovered all. He has spirited her away to Cornwall, to that evil castle! Tintagel! That's where he keeps her. Locked in a high room. With only the sea and the sound of the wind for company.'

'Demand their return,' I tell him.

'The duke?'

'You are the king,' I say. 'It would be treason to refuse.'

'Treason . . .'

Uther nods slowly, raking with a white hand at his beard.

He sends messengers to the west, demanding that the Duke of Cornwall and his wife return immediately to court.

Gorlois sends back the golden cup for answer.

32

King Uther Pendragon takes an army into Cornwall.

He wages war on the duke.

He burns villages. He ravages the Cornish country.

My sorrow, these burnings and ravaging are the outer signs of the lust he feels within.

All Uther Pendragon can think is: Igrayne.

Her name is the name of heaven to him, and the name of hell.

He hears it everywhere.

It mocks him in the wind.

He says it over and over in his dreams.

'Merlin, I must have her.'

'My lord, it is impossible.'

Uther strikes me.

His jewelled glove across my face.

I turn on my heel and leave him to it.

33

Next day. Morning. Columns of mist.

Riding through his camped army, King Uther Pendragon is accosted by an old man.

The old man is mad.

Foam froths from his mouth and his eyes roll in his head.

He catches at Uther's stirrup, crying:

'O the king's needs are known to me!'

'Kill this fool!'

The old man's hand is like a claw round Uther's ankle in its boot.

'You cannot kill me,' he cackles. 'I am the only one who can help the king.'

Uther bends down and snatches at him.

Catching only a handful of mist.

34

A day later. Evening. Dusk falling and snow falling faster.

Riding back from another inconclusive battle with the duke and his followers, King Uther Pendragon is halted by a blind cripple who crouches on his hunkers at the edge of a field of poppies.

'Blind! Blind! Blind!'

'Out of the king's road!'

'But be gentle with him,' Uther commands. 'He has no eyes to see.'

'Blind! Blind! Blind!'

Uther spins his horse.

He says:

'Do not presume too much upon my courtesy.'

The cripple cries:

'It is you who are blind, O king.'

'Cut the fool down!'

'You cannot kill me,' the cripple says. 'I am the only one who can help the king.'

With a leap and a whoop he somersaults and is gone, capering and turning cartwheels through the poppies and the snow, before Uther's men can lay a hand upon him.

35

King Uther Pendragon returns through the snow to his high silk pavilion.

I wait for him there.

'Enchanter,' he says, 'I am glad to see you. I apologize for the blow. I –'

'O blind, blind, blind,' I say.

'And the king's needs are known to me,' I add conversationally, raising my black hat.

'I thought it was you!'

Uther sits down, defeated.

We drink together, late into the night.

'So,' Uther says, 'Merlin is the only one who *can* help the king. And will Merlin be the only one who *does* help the king? What do you say, sorcerer, my friend? I must have the Lady Igrayne. The Lady Igrayne I will have. With your help, I may have her without setting half the kingdom on fire first. Won't you help me to my desire, for the kingdom's sake?'

I stare into the glowing brazier. Its fire is fed with turf, and with sea coals from Lyonnesse.

'Two days I wandered in the green wood,' I say. 'It is where I go when the world overcomes me. In the wood is my mind. In the wood I can wander among my own thoughts, where they are translated into birds and trees. There is order in the growing of a wood. Yes, even in the chaos. For the chaos thrusts through grass, say, and the grass gives it form. I could dine on grass, but never on chaos.'

'Igrayne,' prompts Uther, drinking, and the wine running down in a thin runnel from the corner of his mouth.

'I thought of Igrayne,' I say softly. 'I saw her in the running streams, and in the flowing of the long grass. Her hair was in the shadows of the highest branches, also. She was like the light that dazzles your eyes when you put your hand to your brow and try to stare against the sun in those highest branches. O yes, my lord, I thought of the Lady Igrayne.'

Uther Pendragon says: 'For the kingdom's sake, Merlin.'

'For the kingdom's sake.'

'You will help me? To bed her?'

'For the kingdom's sake.'

'How soon?' demands the king. 'Where? How?'

'Tomorrow night,' I say. 'Tintagel. In the duke's shape.'

Uther catches my wrist. 'I believe you,' he whispers. 'I know you can do anything. O do not doubt, you will be well rewarded.'

'I will,' I say. 'And so will the kingdom. For if I am to assist you to enjoy the Lady Igrayne then you must promise me, now, your hand on this cross, to give me anything I ask you for. Anything at all, without hesitation, so long as it is in your gift to give.'

Uther grasps the crucifix which I extend towards him in the fire's light.

'The king's word,' he promises.

'For the kingdom's sake,' I say, for the third time.

But my eyes, glimpsed suddenly as the moon sails out from a cloud, make Uther Pendragon shiver. Perhaps they are not thinking of the kingdom.

36

The moon. The snow. A man and a girl riding. Two horses on the clifftop. The man on the black horse. The girl on the white.

Tintagel like a castle built of ice above them.

The long sea crashing on the rocks below.

The man and the girl. The black horse and the white. Ascending the winding path to the castle drawbridge.

'Halt!'

A voice softly in the dark, the falling snow.

'Halt! Here are two arrows to take you to your long rest . . .'

The girl whispering.

The man standing up in his stirrups, throwing back his cloak tossing his hair in the moonlight.

He says:

'My compliments upon your watchfulness. But of course you know who it is.'

'My lord?'

'Admit me then.'

The guard calling to his fellow, a fox barking.

'It is the duke.'

'And the woman with him?'

'Nineve.'

'The password.'

'It is the duke!'

'Obtain of him the password, all the same. It is his own instruction.'

'But the duke . . .'

'No one may pass without the word. He would not have it otherwise.'

The man on the black horse calls up to the shadows.

'Quite right to insist upon it, Stilicho. I would not wish you to admit any who did not give you the password. If I do not give you the word known only to us, how can you be sure after all that it is truly me?'

The guard laughs nervously, an owl crying as it winnows through the snow.

'My lord?'

'The word is: *Anima.* Now let me pass, and Nineve also. It's a cold night.'

'It is, my lord.'

The drawbridge clanking down for them. The shadows bringing arrows to their lips in salute as the man and the woman kick their horses to the trot across it. The echo of the horses' hooves sounding sharp against the icy waters of the moat and around the walls of flinty stone.

In the inner courtyard of Tintagel, servants running forward from the massive buttresses, lean shapes sloping in the moonlight across the cobbled snow. The light of torches hand-carried.

Two men bearing lights snatch the heads of the horses.

The man and the girl dismount.

The pair keep their cloaks wrapped close about them as they hurry up flights of steps.

They go in at the door of the tallest tower.

'And my lady?' the man says briefly, as the guard snaps to attention.

'She waits for you, my lord. In the turret room.'

As they ascend the stairs, the girl Nineve says:

'There was no need to ask. I know the way.'

The man says nothing.

His breath comes deeply.

His eyes are hot and hard and very blue.

At the top of the stairs the girl Nineve stops.

She says: 'You go that way. Her door is at the end of the corridor.'

The man goes swiftly in the direction she is pointing. His shadow is everywhere on the walls.

A door painted with stars opening.

The Lady Igrayne saying:

'My lord?'

Igrayne is wearing a nightdress of thin white silk. Her hair is braided up upon her head, but one braid hangs loose and she brushes it back with a sleepy hand as the other hand holds the door.

Then he is into the room, and her arms go around him, and her mouth meets his mouth where it seeks her, and the door shuts.

37

The girl Nineve stands a moment in the corridor. Then she moves. She goes like a ghost, or one sleep-walking. It is as if her red slippers have a doom in them which she cannot avoid. There is a compulsion to her movement. What she is doing is not necessarily what she wants to do, but it has been ordained and predestined and she does it. And some dark part of her wants it too, and hastens to the consummation.

The wall of the long corridor is covered by a tapestry.

A forest scene.

Over-arching leafy trees, deer feeding, a unicorn among the cedars. Through the underwoods a glimpse of a pool in the far distance. Its surface is like steel made blue by fire.

The girl Nineve *steps into the tapestry.*

One moment she is in the long corridor of Tintagel, the next she is walking down the avenue of cedars in the tapestry.

It is green in the painted forest.

It is green and cool and no birds sing.

There's not a breath of wind in the painted forest.

There is brightness from the painted sun, but that sun gives no heat.

Nineve walks on. Her footfalls are like heartbeats.

The trees of the forest have roots as deep as their branches are high.

Nineve walks on. She walks deep in the forest. She has come to the place where all is shadow.

Nineve steps into the glade of shadows.

The glade is oak trees on three sides, including the side through which Nineve has stepped in entering it. The trees are close together. Very little light trickles down through their entwined branches. There is a stillness and a heaviness, a threat of thunder in the unmoving air.

The fourth side of the glade is solid glass.

The other side of the glass is no doubt a mirror, but this side you can see through as through a sheet of solid ice held up against the daylight from the top of a well in winter.

Nineve stands still.

She catches her breath.

The girl's little breasts move up and down eagerly under the thin soft stuff of her dress as she takes in the scene on the other side of the glass wall in the forest.

The mirror looks into the turret room of the Lady Igrayne.

It is a long, low, oval room, hung with tapestries of scarlet and yellow, and paved with black and white marble.

The ceiling of that room is painted with stars. There is Orion, there the Pleiades. The only symbol disfiguring a scene of perfect astronomical accuracy is the presence in the same night sky of *two moons*. One moon rises easterly, full, blood-bedimmed, furious. The other moon wanes in the west, a leprous crescent.

The floor of the room is strewn with green rushes.

The air is thick with the blue vapour of some perfume burning in a copper brazier.

The room is lit by lamps suspended from the walls, their lights glowing from behind screens of a pure pink silk.

Under the ceiling of painted stars the room's only other furniture is a vast white bed, half-masked by a coverlet made of black damask.

On that bed lies the Lady Igrayne.

She is naked save for a pair of silver slippers.

Above her towers the man she takes for her husband. His

body is hard and muscly, his chest and his legs covered with thick black hair. He is quite naked save for his riding boots.

His member is huge and hard as he towers above her.

He has a black whip in his fist.

Igrayne's white body has one mark across it already.

She lies on her back, her hair outspread beneath her.

Her eyes look up adoringly at the man.

Her hands reach out for that throbbingly upright member.

The girl Nineve is watching every move. She finds the scene disturbing. Here, for her secret approval, he is enacting the very picture which she created in his head. It is as if a private fantasy has suddenly been given shape and substance in some erotic theatre of the soul where all desires are fulfilled and every dream made actual. *To keep her in order?*

The whip comes down.

Its thin black thong bites into Igrayne's breasts, leaving a red kiss like a devil's mark across them.

She wriggles upon the bed, offering her husband the freedom of her buttocks.

The whip comes down.

It whistles in the air no doubt, though Nineve cannot hear it through the glass. It makes a sharp music also as it punishes the firm white flesh of Igrayne's bottom.

There is nothing to hear, but plenty to see.

The whip comes up and the whip comes down.

The man is whipping the Lady Igrayne thoroughly on her bare buttocks.

And the Lady Igrayne loves it.

She rolls and tosses on the black damask coverlet. She is panting. Her lips are twisted in some expression of ecstasy – perhaps a scream, but the thick glass wall muffles all sound completely and Nineve hears nothing.

The girl can see Igrayne's flesh getting redder and redder, though, as her husband whips her. And she watches as Igrayne's lips apparently cry out her hot wish for him to whip her harder, harder, harder still.

The man obliges.

The whip comes up and the whip comes down.

The sweat flies from him.

But Igrayne seems insatiable for the whip.

She needs it. She deserves it. She must have it.

Her body is as firm and white as marble. Under the whip it has grown like marble inflamed. She thrusts herself up and down and from side to side as she takes her sweet chastisement.

Now the hands of the Lady Igrayne are reaching once more for her husband's member.

She is kneeling on the bed, her hair like an autumn waterfall about her. He shoulders, her back, her buttocks – all are marked with the kiss of the whip.

Igrayne takes her husband's prick in her hands.

His prick is long and hard, like a little sword. But Igrayne's hands are longer, and her fingers are wise. She runs them up and down the flesh that fascinates her. It quivers, red and rude. She rubs it.

There is a pearl of sperm in the eye of the duke's prick.

He stands stock still as his wife inches slowly down upon him across the bed.

The Lady Igrayne buries her face in her husband's groin.

Her unbraided hair, auburn, flowing, is all across his private parts.

She licks her lips.

She kisses his prick.

She kisses it again and again, plainly enjoying the way it leaps like a salmon under the work of her hot red lips.

She runs her tongue up and down it, kittenishly. Meanwhile playing and fiddling with it the more.

Then the Lady Igrayne looks up at her husband longingly.

He nods, touching her cheek with the whip.

Igrayne takes his prick in her mouth, and sucks.

Nineve sees the muscles working in Igrayne's swan-like neck. She has the knob of her husband's organ in her lips, and she is sucking it hard, but it is not enough for her.

She nibbles his prick hungrily, thirstily, then she is gobbling for more, for more, for more, and her whole greedy mouth is over it, taking more erect and throbbing flesh into her suck than Nineve would have believed was possible.

Not that the girl Nineve has ever seen anything quite like this, or even imagined such a scene in any such detail.

The Lady Igrayne is sucking and sucking at her husband's huge cock, while her delicate long fingers touch and caress his balls, stroking, playing, urging, and chase also around and around the root of the organ which is giving her mouth such pleasure.

The man she takes for the duke kneels above her now, dark on the white sheets, and dark and hairy against the smooth white flesh of his attentive young wife.

He thrusts the whip down to touch her sex.

Igrayne's legs come together over it, folding it in her embrace, like the wings of a swan.

One silver slipper falls off.

She remains a moment, coiled, poised, her thighs pressed tight to feel the thrust of the whip, her mouth still sucking with unsatisfiable longing at her husband's prick.

Then he forces her down on her back, and falls upon her, rising and falling, rising and falling, plunging.

And the man and the woman roll locked together across the bed, Igrayne's body bucking to take the thrust of him, greedy to have the full worth of his iron-hard prick inside her, where it is doing most damage of pleasure, in the dark sleek grove of her cunt.

Nineve sees a sword thrust into a stone, a lance thrust bleeding into a golden cup. A voice in her head cries: *Whom does this Grail serve?* She does not know the answer.

38

'And Sir Perceval came to the Castle of Wonders,' says the devil my father. 'The gate of the castle was open, and when he came to the hall that door was open also, and Sir Perceval went in. And he saw a great chessboard in that hall, and the chessmen moving square to square to square, playing against each other, by themselves. And Sir Perceval favoured the white side, but they lost the game, and thereupon the black pieces set up a shout of triumph as if they had been living men. And this angered Sir Perceval, so that he swept the chessmen into his lap, black and white, and cast the great chessboard into the sea.'

39

'And Sir Perceval grinned,' say my uncle Astarot and my uncle Beelzebub together, 'Sir Perceval grinned like a fox eating shit out of a wire brush.'

40

The girl Nineve and the man in the shape of the Duke of Cornwall are riding as though my father the devil himself is at their heels.

They spur their horses.

The black horse and the white horse galloping.

As though their riders' whole desire is to put as much distance as possible between themselves and the castle of Tintagel.

Galloping over snow.

Galloping under a vast sky that is paling for the dawn. Faint pale clouds clustered round the dying moon.

At last, the horses stop, ridden out.

Stand, shivering, to rest in a swift-flowing stream.

The black horse and the white.

And the man turns to Nineve and says:

'Damn you.'

And then, in the next breath:

'Thank you.'

The girl Nineve looks at her reflection in the water.

Her face is flowing away.

Quick fishes dart through it, like thoughts, like shadows.

Her eyes are the eyes of someone who has looked into hell and seen themself there.

She says:

'There will be a time to say thank you. When the child is born, you are to give it to me.'

The man frowns with fear.

'I see. For what devil's reason?'

'None,' says the girl Nineve. 'He will one day be king.'

The man dismounts.

He washes his hands in the river. He thrusts his fists through it and through it, as though striking blows at an invisible adversary.

'For the kingdom's sake, eh?' the man shouts in such a loud voice that the snow-filled forest rings with his words.

The girl says nothing.

She stares at her face in the water.

Her eyes regret what they see.

More, little pig. They hate it.

She flings herself from the horse's back and plunges her arms into the river, destroying the hateful image. She throws handfuls of water over her face, rubbing at it, scrubbing at it, as if to wash it clean of all the sins that have marked it since the first cleansing waters of baptism.

The man stands, waist-deep, watching her.

Then he too starts to scrub at his face with the water.

In a little while, I, Merlin, confront King Uther Pendragon in the flowing river. I still wear the girl's green gown and the king is still garbed in the black ermines of the Duke of Cornwall. We stare at each other, the splashed water trickling down our faces.

The king smiles nervously.

I look at him.

We wade from the river.

We have thrown our cloaks about us, hiding our strange attire, and ridden a little way farther in the direction of the camp, when a party of Pendragon's horsemen meet us crying that the Duke of Cornwall is dead and the war is won.

'How?' says the king.

'Last night, my lord. He made a sudden sortie from the Castle Terrible, and was struck down by an axe.'

'Who wielded the axe?' says Uther.

The men look up and down the snow-filled ways.

Then one of them says uncomfortably:

'The strange thing, my lord – no one is sure. This one says it was that one, that one says it was another. No one claims responsibility for the duke's death.'

Uther shrugs. 'Well,' he says. 'He *is* dead.'

'O yes. He is dead.'

We ride on in silence as the sun climbs in the sky.

The forest all around is white with snow.

Then I tell King Uther Pendragon:

'You killed him. With Igrayne.'

The Red Book

1

My uncle the prince Beelzebub says:

'I don't like it.'

'I'm not happy about it either,' says my uncle Astarot. 'I can't understand a half of it, to tell you the truth. It seems to have got out of hand.'

'I don't like the complications,' Beelzebub says. 'I like stories. It's a good plain story. Can't we let it be?'

My father the devil says nothing.

He is busy grooming the dog Cerberus.

His long green face wears an expression of unalterable boredom.

'Take the end of that chapter where Uther fucked Igrayne,' says Astarot, an uncommon thoughtfulness creasing his bricky red face. 'What was happening there exactly? What did Merlin do? What was being done to him? What does it all *mean*?'

'It seemed obscure to me also,' my uncle Beelzebub says.

My father giggles.

He has a bone in each hand.

The grooming ended, he is feeding the dog.

But Cerberus has three heads, and the third head snaps and spits at the other two as they gnaw the bones.

'I'm surprised,' says my father. 'Surprised and disappointed.' He wipes his hands on his blasting rod. 'Just when things start to go along *very* nicely, you two girls have to come on complaining and carping. I don't mind complaints. Much. But I'll ask you kindly not to carp.' He waves the blasting rod to make his point. 'Cease carping. Forthwith. Thank you.'

My father the devil giggles again.

'We have young Merlin where we want him now,' he says.

'Now we know his weakness. Not precisely an Achilles' *heel*, but . . .'

'You mean he could be one of ours?' my uncle A asks, disbelievingly.

'Not exactly,' says my father. 'Not exactly that, no. O no, I don't think that could ever be, *quite*. But there's enough here of weakness and error to turn the plot to our liking.'

My uncle Beelzebub offers a third bone to the dog Cerberus, to put it out of its self-destroying misery.

The dog bites him.

'Plot?' says uncle B, howling.

And:

'Liking?' howls uncle B, nursing his fanged fingers.

'You make it all sound like a book,' my uncle Astarot says for him.

'Everything is a book,' my father says.

2

I am a candle in the bedroom of the Lady Igrayne.

Be sure, little pig, she has no need to use me as that abbess Dame Pudicity used her candles.

For King Uther Pendragon married the Lady Igrayne some few nights after he had lain with her. (She missed her husband, and was not reluctant.) And ever since that time the Lady Igrayne has not lacked for company.

I like to watch them at it.

Myself unseen, I like to watch their love games.

It is six months since their wedding, and the king has pleasured her every night in one way or another, but she is still as greedy for it.

And I am still greedier to see what they do.

I love to watch him doing it to her, and to see her done.

Merlin the watcher.

Sometimes I am a spider on the wall, or a book by the bed, or a gleam of water reflected on the ceiling above them. Once (O happy once, my sweetness, my friend) I was the sheet beneath the Lady Igrayne's back, and the king thrust at both of us. I rubbed her bottom as he came in her. I was stuck between her wet thighs as she came.

Being a sheet has its disadvantages, however.

As a candle, you can at least burn when you feel like it.

So tonight I am a flaming candle as he buggers her.

In the midst of the buggering, King Uther Pendragon says:

'And who is the father of the child?'

'My lord?'

'Who is the child's father?'

Igrayne shuts her eyes. There are tears in them.

'That was witchcraft,' she says. 'On the night that the duke died, in the very hour of his death, as I heard, his ghost came to me in my tower at Tintagel, and begot the child upon me.'

'A ghost?'

'Yes, my lord.'

'A ghost did *this* to you?'

'Not this, my lord. The other.'

Uther chuckles and grunts, busy upon her bum.

'Can a ghost have left you with child?' he says. 'Isn't it some devil's spawn that's in your womb?'

Igrayne buries her head in the pillow.

She opens her eyes wide but the tears do not move in them.

She stares at me where I burn by the bedside.

Her face is a flame of delight at what her husband is doing to her rear passage.

'My lord,' she gasps, in rhythm with his thrustings. 'My lord . . . My lord . . . My lord . . .'

The king withdraws.

He says:

'Since the child is not mine, by your own confession, but the dead duke's devil-child, you must promise me that it will be delivered secretly.'

Igrayne says nothing.

She rubs the cheeks of her behind against him, seeking to re-engage the thing she needs.

Uther goes on talking, coldly:

'And you must promise me also that the child will be disposed of as I shall direct.'

The Lady Igrayne looks round at him over her shoulder.

'This is Merlin's doing,' she says softly. 'Merlin is at the root of this evil.'

Her husband smacks her bottom with his prick.

'Merlin wants the child,' he says, 'so Merlin must have it. Promise me that. Promise me that – or you'll have no more of this!'

The Lady Igrayne laughs and the tears run down her face.

Then she says:

'I promise.'

And then she says:

'. . . My lord!'

3

The Lady Igrayne's baby is covered with hair.

4

'Wait!' cries my uncle Astarot. 'Let's get this straight. Just hold it there! Do we mean to imply some correspondence between Igrayne's baby just born and the child of the virgin Vivien? I mean to say – *covered with hair* . . . Merlin was like that until they went and baptized him twice. You mean to say you got into Uther getting into the Duke of Cornwall? Into his prick? You mean *you* fucked her?'

My father winces with distaste as he considers his lieutenant over a bowl of maggots.

'No,' he says.

'No what—' says my uncle Astarot, pouring cognac on the maggots.

'No, not at all,' says my father. 'Nothing so crude, nothing so obvious as what you suggest. I'll never be *that* reduced again, I thank you. Never so carnal, so brief, so cut down to the size of *their* caperings and couplings. No. But be sure there's a bit of it in every human congress.'

He drinks the maggots, my daddy.

'Of what?' says my uncle Beelzebub.

'Of us!' says my uncle Astarot. 'Of *evil*, eh, Shiner?'

'Glory,' sighs my father, 'why can't I have angelic henchmen? Why do I have to suffer idiots and crudities?'

My uncle Beelzebub is buzzing through his teeth. Something in the tilt of his head suggests an alchemist bending over a retort. 'Calumniator, I began to understand,' he says. 'It is implied that the union of Igrayne and Uther, bizarre and wrenched and violent as it was, through Igrayne's lusts and Uther's lie (his shape shift, his transformation), is in essence an evil act – and that from this invocation of our powers there is again the possibility of the Antichrist?'

'Almighty Sod!' says Astarot. 'He right?'

'And what does that make Merlin?' Beelzebub goes on. 'Why, a midwife to Antichrist, a sort of foster father – for hasn't he demanded the child of Uther?'

My uncle Astarot's eyes cloud with the possibility of understanding. 'You mean he *does* want the child for our purposes?' he says.

My father licks his lips.

His tongue is like a hook.

'All purposes are my purpose,' he says.

And then:

'There is no escape from the net I have about Merlin's feet. It is in any case a silken net of his own weaving. That is the point of the story.'

'But the Grail?' says my uncle Beelzebub.

'A toy,' says my father. 'A toy for knights, poets and children.'

'And his talk of the kingdom?' uncle B goes on.

'Ah,' says my father the devil. 'The kingdom, the kingdom ... A vague enough term. For Thine is the kingdom ... Shall we take it that when Merlin talks about the kingdom he refers not to some temporal region or time of their world, but to a kingdom where eternal Sorrow reigns.'

'Sorrow?' say my uncles as one devil.

'The old, endless, approachable and always answering Sorrow,' says my father Lucifer. 'For who calls on me never goes unanswered. Only prayers to God go without answers.'

5

'There's this knight,' says my uncle Astarot. 'His name is Sir Gawain. He's young. He's handsome. He's tall. He's dressed in a surcoat of red satin and a mantle of crimson, trimmed with gold. On his head there's a cap of rich purple. His feet and legs are clad in fine leather. Gold bosses on his shoes. Well, he meets this damsel weeping by a fountain, see? She's lovely. A gentle womanly dignity in her voice. A steady stately walk. A real queen. Her thighs are warm and glossy. If you laid a ruler against her feet, it would be hard to find any fault with them. Now, Sir Gawain is looking for the Holy Grail. So naturally he refuses to have intercourse with her. The damsel is very impressed. This is the first knight who ever met her weeping by this fountain who didn't have her down on her back and her knickers off in fifteen minutes. So she says to Sir Gawain: "Good knight, I will do for you what I have never done for any knight before. *Have you heard of the Sleeve Job?*" '

'Enough!' shrieks my father.

6

'When Merlin meets the one who watched King Uther Pendragon beating the Lady Igrayne,' my father the devil says, 'when Merlin pleasures the one who was so pleasured by the sight of that – *then* we shall have him for ever . . .'

'Wait!' cries uncle Astarot. 'What one can that be? Wasn't *he* watching?'

'In drag,' says uncle Beelzebub.

'Ah, ladies,' sighs my father, 'he is a man of power, that Merlin, that spoiled Antichrist, but he is my son also . . . The meaning of all corn is wheat, and of all metals gold, and of all births that of man.'

7

My head aches too, apple tree, little apple tree, my sweetness, my friend, my daughter.

If I could understand my father's words at this point in the story then perhaps the end would not be as it must be.

What end?

I am in the Grail Castle.

I am the Grail Keeper.

All I eat is the host that is brought to me on the large gold platter guarded by the bleeding lance.

I have been maimed.

Wounded through the thighs. The genitals.

By my own sacred sword.

Few come. Fewer go.

This castle is enveloped in mist, and hidden from the sight of those who search for it. To reach it, you must seem to ride away. In the opposite direction, that is.

If you arrive here, if you see the Grail procession – the lady with the platter, the bleeding lance, me on the litter – then there is the matter of the question.

The Quest and then the question.

The question that must be asked to heal the king, and make the land to bloom again.

The question that will heal me.

King Merlin.

In my green prison.

In this esplumoir.

Hung here in a cage between one world and another.

8

The night. The path. The silence.

I am at the postern gate.

In the rags of a beggar.

Igrayne has brought her baby down to me.

It is all done secretly.

Only Igrayne and Uther and myself know of the child's existence.

Or so I think until the moment when the door closes and I turn away from the postern, the child in my arms, to face the night, the path, and the silence.

Then I feel her eyes observing me.

I turn.

There is no one there.

But as I go away down the path, with the child wrapped in my cloak, I know who is watching me. The other witness to the child's existence.

Morgan le Fay.

Little Morgan, the Lady Igrayne's daughter by her previous husband, the Duke of Cornwall.

Somewhere, at one of the windows in the dark castle, little Morgan is watching me.

She knows.

She is a knowing child.

Her eyes burn upon my back as I go away down the steep path, into the night, the silence.

I bear the baby into the green wood.

The trees our chapel.

A waterfall our font.

I baptize him with wild water:

'In the name of the Father and of the Son and of the Holy Ghost:

Arthur.'

9

So first I came to you, my tree, my sweetness. Though not as now.

Not as now, when first I saw you.

You sprang with gentle flowers, growing hidden in the woodlands. Sweet apple tree which grows on a river bank.

Was I mad, when first I saw you?

Merlin mad.

Merlin the wild man.

Yes, little sweetness. Merlin has been mad since the night when he watched Uther and Igrayne for the first time.

In days of old, when knights were two a penny.

Merlin the demigod.

Roaming in the wild wood.

Merlin the green man.

Eating frozen moss, and grass, and leaves, and roots.

I have a cave in the forest. No one knows it. There is an ash tree this side of it, and a hazel on the other. My lintel is of honeysuckle.

The size of my cave is small yet not small.

A little lowly hidden cave.

Will you come with me to see it, little pig?

O little pig, I do not sleep easily.

From the agitation of the sorrow which is upon me.

For ten and forty years I have suffered pain.

My appearance is woeful.

Snow up to my hips among the forest wolves.

Icicles in my hair, spent is my splendour.

Years pass like this.

Excellent clear springs. A cup of water, splendid to drink.

Yew berries. Bird cherries.

Foxes on the green grass round the mouth of my cave.

The boyhood of Arthur.

10

My brothers, the fur peeled off him when I baptized him in the waterfall.

Arthur.

You have been warned.

11

The boyhood of Arthur. The madness of Merlin.

Look.

A golden-haired boy running through a deep golden pool of sunlight falling into the trees in the deepest deep of the wild green wood.

Arthur running through the golden in the green.

His golden hair. His green tunic.

'Sometimes you seem mad, or a fool, or a boy like me.'

'The knower of truth should go about the world outwardly stupid. Like a child, a madman, or a devil.'

12

Tall deer, does, a badger's brood.

Fruits of rowan, sloes of the blackthorn.

Pignuts in summer, and marjoram. The cresses of the stream. Green purity!

Swarms of bees, and Arthur running.

Woodpeckers with their pied hoods, through the golden.

His hair. His tunic.

His flashing feet.

13

I teach him. Merlin teaches Arthur.

'To learn anything well, one must forget it several times.'

'The sign expresses the thing.'

'The thing is the virtue of the sign.'

'There is an analogical correspondence between the sign and the thing signified.'

'The more perfect is the sign, the more entire is the correspondence.'

'To say a word is to evoke a thought and make it present. To name God is to manifest God.'

'The word acts upon souls, and souls react upon bodies; consequently one can frighten, console, cause to fall ill, cure, even kill, and raise from the dead by means of words.'

'To utter a name is to create or evoke a being.'

'In the name is contained the verbal or spiritual doctrine of the being itself.'

'When the soul evokes a thought, the sign of that thought is written automatically in the light.'

'To invoke is to adjure. That is to say, to swear by a name. It is to perform an act of faith in that name, and to communicate in the virtue which it represents.'

'Words in themselves are, then, good or evil, poisonous or wholesome.'

'The most dangerous words are vain and lightly uttered words, because they are the voluntary abortions of thought.'

'A useless word is a crime against the spirit of intelligence. It is an intellectual infanticide.'

'Things are for every one what he makes of them by naming them. The *word* of every one is an impression or an habitual prayer.'

'To speak well is to live well.'

'A fine style is an aureole of holiness.'

14

I teach him. Merlin teaches Arthur.

To KNOW.

To DARE.

To WILL.

To KEEP SILENT.

Arthur is not a good pupil.

15

Years pass like this. Fifteen winters, if you want to know. Merlin mad in the green wood, yes, but far away in Logres I watch the reign of King Uther Pendragon. There is a pool in the forest, a pool where bright-breasted ring-doves bathe in summer and where in winter a dark torrent issues from the rocks. It is in this pool that I watched Pendragon's fate. My hand whirls the water. In the changing patterns I see what befalls the king.

Look.

The lady Igrayne stripped of her shift by another man.

Her lover is the King of Orkney, Lot.

Uther suspects his wife's unfaithfulness, but cannot prove it.

As men do, who are so tormented, he falls ill at last of wasting sickness.

Look.

The king's days are numbered by his physicians.

Uther lies white and impotent in his bed.

Igrayne laughs in the arms of the King of Orkney.

He has a big prick. It is all she cares about.

Not so, my sorrow. She cares about malevolence also.

She casts about, seeking to find the thing that will hurt her husband most.

A fly speaks in her ear.

She finds it.

She gives away the Round Table, making a gift of it to her lover.

Uther is powerless to prevent her.

Lot sets the table on the Orkney shore.

He sits down at it and eats his dinner looking out to sea.

The tide comes in and laps around his ankles.

Lot, King of Orkney, grins like a fox eating shit out of a wire brush.

16

Little Jesus, now things start happening fast.

Observing King Uther Pendragon on his deathbed in my autumn pool, his dying face among the drifting leaves, I set out for Camelot in Logres.

I travel alone.

Arthur I leave in company with a widowed knight called Auctor, who lives in a ramshackle castle on the edge of the forest.

'But he can't stay here for ever,' Auctor warns me. 'Come Christmas and I take my son Kay to camelot, to be made a knight.'

'Excellent,' I say. 'Bring Arthur with you then.'

Three days from Camelot I hear Uther's dead.

I ride on, my chin on my chest, the October wind a punishment in my hair.

Two days from Camelot I hear that Igrayne has fled with her daughter Morgan. No one knows where.

I ride on, through the wind and the rain, my cloak like a black wing behind me.

One day from Camelot I learn that Igrayne has gone to the side of the King of Orkney, Lot, and that together they plan to bring the Saxons in and have the throne for themselves.

I ride on, plotting furiously in my head.

17

I come to Camelot.

'You are too late,' they tell me. 'Uther is dead.'

'Where is he? Let me see him!'

'But he is dead. You are too late.'

I smile. I flick my fingers.

'To bring the dead to life,' I say, 'is no great magic. Is the king buried yet?'

'No.'

'Then bring me to him.'

Six barons escort me to the chamber where the body lies. King Uther Pendragon is in his shroud. The room smells foul.

'You see? You believe us now? The king is dead.'

I stand in the doorway.

I strike the ground three times with my staff.

'Uther!' I shout. 'Uther Pendragon! Who is to be king? Shall Igrayne rule? And Orkney?'

King Uther Pendragon rises up in his shroud.

His bandaged jaw breaks open.

'Never!' he cries.

And then his black and rotting lips proclaim:

'The king is dead. Long live the king!'

I nod.

'Who *is* the king?' I ask him.

'My son is the king,' says Uther.

And falls back dead in the pool of his own putrescence.

18

All that is mortal of King Uther Pendragon is buried beside his brother Aurelius Ambrosius in the ring of the Giants' Dance at Stonehenge.

The six barons have scarcely kicked the last clod of earth down upon his coffin before they start arguing among themselves concerning the succession.

'Merlin is mad.'

'He brought the dead king to life.'

'Correction. He *seemed* to bring the dead king to life. Which is of course impossible.'

'Witchcraft. It was witchcraft.'

'Whatever it was, however he did it, I heard with my own ears the king cry out that his son should succeed him.'

'So what? He has no son.'

'But Merlin was satisfied with that saying of the king's. I saw his face. He let the king rest in peace after.'

'Merlin is mad.'

'Grief, his grief. He loved the king.'

'He is old now also, and out of his wits.'

'He is not old. I saw him riding. But sometimes he looks old, as old as the trees in the green wood, as old as the forests.'

'Merlin is as old as the forests, yes. He belongs out there. His wits have gone with his years in the forests, living among wild beasts. He knows nothing.'

I hear them, my friend wolf.

I stare at a kestrel riding the wind over Stonehenge, and I hear the barons' voices as if I stood in the heart of their debate.

At last they come to me, more out of fear than respect.

'We don't want Igrayne and Lot. They will bring in the Saxons. What shall we do?'

'Wait and pray,' I tell them.

'. . .?'

'Wait until Christmas,' I tell them. 'And pray that God sends the rightful king.'

19

Now I see the cunning of the Lady Igrayne in giving the Round Table to her lover.

For the kingdom is divided, and there are those who say that Lot should be crowned King of all Britain simply because he has the Table.

Even some of the barons favour this opinion.

Word of the dead king's final speech has spread through

Logres and beyond, however. (I saw to this, O Jesukin.) Consequently there are just as many people who hold that Uther's son is the rightful heir, and who believe that this unknown son will manifest himself when the right time comes.

Meanwhile, I brush up my swordsmanship.

It has grown rusty in the green wood, with only the boy Arthur for my opponent.

So I practise. Startling the barons who believe me old.

And hear that the eighteen-year-old Morgan le Fay has been delivered to a nunnery.

20

'At last,' says my father, blowing perfect triangles of smoke and laughing like a clock running down at the same time.

'Triangles?' says my uncle Astarot.

'Full possession again!' says my father. 'Better than Blaise and Pudicity ... There has to be a *will* to accommodate. And here it comes! A will, a home, a wish, a longing ... I never saw a more perfect specimen. Such evil! Such beauty!'

'*Who?*' says Astarot, interested by my father's unusual enthusiasm. 'Is it Igrayne? Has she come over to us utterly? Of course we already had her by the roots. It can't be ... Is it her?'

My father says:

'Igrayne is only fit for whipping. Igrayne's soul is passive. She is a sensuous little nothing. She is acted upon, she does not act. She did the will of the Duke of Cornwall, which was to some degree ours. Then she did Uther's will, ditto but less. Now she is doing the will of our willing servant Lot – with some promptings from the lord of the diptera, bless him.'

'Aha,' says uncle Astarot, 'it's Orkney then?'

'No,' cries my father, writhing with pleasure on a prong of fire. 'Not at all. No way!'

'*Who* then?'

'Morgan,' says my father.

'Morgan le Fay!'

'Morgan, as you say, le Fay!' my father exults. 'For years I have felt very close to little Morgan. Now she is about to make the invocation! Her will and my will! *Here it comes!*'

21

'Emperor Lucifer,' prays Morgan le Fay, down on her knees in the chapel of the convent of the Flaming Heart, 'master and prince of rebellious spirits, I adjure thee to leave thine abode, in whatsoever quarter of the world it may be situated, and come hither to communicate with me. I command and I conjure thee in the name of the mighty living God (Father ✠ Son ✠ and Holy Ghost ✠) to appear without noise and without any evil smell, to respond in a clear and intelligible voice, point by point, to all that I ask thee, failing which, thou shalt be most surely compelled to obedience by the power of the divine ADONAI, ELOIM, ARIEL, JEHOVAM, TAGLA, MATHON, and by the whole hierarchy of superior intelligences, who shall constrain thee against thy will. *Venite, venite*!'

22

'Divine!' says my daddy. 'Exquisite, dear. Thanks!'

'You're not appearing to her?' Astarot asks.

'Of course I'm not appearing to her. Let her wonder for a while if I exist! The point is – Morgan le Fay will make this story ours! *Morgan le Fay is writing this story now!*'

23

Here we go again, my brothers. Quite, quite fantastic. Absurd as hell.

Let me make it quite clear to the doubtful:

This book has one maker and one maker only.

Who ever heard of a book being written by the characters in it?

I tell you about my father. I tell you about Morgan le Fay.

I say it as I see it, little pig.

Of course, there is a sense in which Morgan le Fay could be said to be writing *her* story, and my father the devil is writing *his* story, and Arthur so, and Igrayne so, and all the rest of them who have an original and autonomous existence apart from me.

But that is not what my father means.

He is forever pretending, the devil, that the world is his work.

He is the enemy of free will.

All I know is that the same event goes on happening.

A nun whips a virgin. A king whips a wanton. A white worm defeats a red worm. A devil claims dominion.

And I am in Glass Castle, in the spiral vortex, in the turning glass grave or green alchemical retort where Mercurius must resolve the complexities of Merlin, where gold must be made of base metals, and where I must make sense of myself.

On with the process! Follow the dance!

24

'Ite missa est . . .'

Says the archbishop of Canterbury.

The bells ring out.

The bells ring out across the roofs of Logres.

Red roofs and towers under the night sky.

Snow starts falling.

Big soft flakes. Like feathers from the wings of a great white bird.

A swan. An albatross. A swan.

Snow falling and falling.

Dismissed at the end of the midnight mass of Christmas, the barons and the knights pour out, a glittering company, down the porphyry stair of Saint Paul's.

Carols on the midnight air. A party of carol singers with a lantern.

'Let them gather cherries . . .'

The carol dies upon their lips.

'Look! Look!'

The barons and the knights shout out in wonder.

There, in the churchyard, in the falling snow, a great square slab of milk-white marble.

And in the marble an anvil of iron.

And set point downwards in the iron a shining sword!

And round about the anvil these words written in letters of gold:

WHOSO PULLS OUT THIS SWORD FROM THIS STONE IS BORN THE RIGHTFUL KING OF ALL BRITAIN.

How's that for high?

25

Did I put it there, my Jesus?

Are you joking?

Did I put it there?

You realize what you're saying!

You know my penchant for swords . . .

Who the hell else *could* have put it there?

Uncle Astarot.

Uncle Beelzebub.

Ah, they only do what my daddy tells them.

I promise you they have nothing to do with this.

26

'The sword is in the stone,' my father says. 'Thank you, Morgan le Fay!'

27

There he goes again! The fictioneer!

He makes me mad.

The devil!

The arch anti-plotter!
Bugger it up he will, if he can.
There's no stopping him.
Yet.
Just wait!
Just wait and see.
We're nearer now than once we were to the point that is soon enough reached.
Daddy! Daddy! I've seen you leering in the lavatories!

28

Brothers mine, I grant you this. Morgan le Fay has nothing to do with the sword in the stone. But she *may* have to do with Arthur's delay in arriving at Logres. For the first time, my knowledge of the shining twit's not perfect. Something clouds the crystal, befogs the issue, and I cannot see. It is my intuition that Igrayne's daughter has a touch to do with this, but *how*, and *where*, when Arthur is in Auctor's castle and Morgan in the convent of the Flaming Heart – that is a matter I cannot explain.

Meanwhile, there is the comedy of the barons' quarrel.
'Me first!'
'Over my dead body!'
And so on.
It takes a sermon from the archbishop of Canterbury to sort them out. They accept the order of precedence which he recommends.
None of them succeeds in drawing the sword, of course.

29

New Year comes, and Arthur comes to Logres. He journeys in company with Sir Auctor and his son Kay. Ostensibly their delay has been due to the death of King Uther Pendragon. Kay was to come to Camelot to be knighted, do you remember?

Now there is no king to knight him, so no real need for his journey. However, father and son are riding to the tournament which is held in Logres on every New Year's Day, and they bring Arthur with them as Kay's squire.

Riding to the jousts, Kay realizes that he has left his sword in his lodgings.

'Will you ride back and fetch it for me?'

'I will.'

Arthur might not be bright, but he always was obliging.

When he gets to the lodgings, though, the door is locked. Everyone is at the tournament.

I think you know the rest, O Jesukin?

Ask me nothing you can guess.

How Arthur, passing the churchyard, sees the sword in the stone.

How the guardians of the sword have gone to the tournament also. So that no one sees the boy draw the sword from the stone.

How Arthur takes the sword to Kay, and Kay recognizes it, and rides instantly to his father, and says:

'Sir, here is the sword out of the stone. So you see I must be the rightful king of all Britain!'

And how Sir Auctor rides back with Kay and Arthur to the churchyard, and bids his son with his hand on the great Bible to tell him truly how he came by the sword.

'Sir, the truth is: Arthur brought it to me.'

Sir Auctor wheels. 'And how did you come by it?'

'I pulled it from the stone,' says Arthur.

'Then put it back,' Sir Auctor instructs him, doubtfully, 'and let me see you draw it out again.'

'Easy meat,' says Arthur, raising his arm and stabbing the sword back again into the stone, where it sticks quivering as before.

And Sir Auctor cannot draw it out.

And his son Kay cannot draw it out.

But Arthur draws it out again as easily as if the sword is coming from a well-greased scabbard.

And how Sir Auctor kneels before him, calling him king.

'God save King Arthur!'
God save us all.

30

Not all the barons like the idea though.

'Wolf boy from the woods.'

'Merlin's bastard brat.'

I hear them.

I say nothing.

I stand in my cloak in the falling snow, my black hat pulled down at the brim.

I let them put things off till Candlemas.

Ten knights watch over the sword by day and by night.

At Candlemas, the knights and the barons try their strength again.

It is as it was.

No one can draw the sword save only Arthur.

'Again at Easter!'

Easter comes. The snow is melted. The daisies star the grass. Only Arthur can draw the sword from the stone.

'Till Pentecost!'

They hope all the time that some great champion will be found, who can draw the sword and discredit the claims of this boy.

But at Pentecost it is the same old story.

Arthur draws the sword from the stone again.

Arthur alone can draw the sword from the stone.

Then all the common men cry out:

'Arthur! We will have Arthur! By God's will he is our king! Long live King Arthur!'

And they kneel before him, rich and poor together, and ask his mercy because they ever doubted him.

And Arthur forgives them, and lays the sword on the altar of Saint Paul's and is crowned king.

The creep.

31

While Morgan le Fay fashions a stone effigy of her mother the Lady Igrayne, and then thrusts a sword through the heart of it, by some magic almost the equal of mine, and then usurps her mother's place in King Lot's bed – for Igrayne falls down dead, struck through the heart, and Morgan marries her stepfather, and now she is crowned Queen Morgan le Fay and lies abed beside Lot, and both of them grin like foxes eating shit out of a wire brush.

32

'Camelot in Logres,' I tell King creepy Arthur. 'Let Camelot be a castle built to music. A castle set in meadows full of light. Let it be perfectly spaced, and plentifully watered. Arcaded also, and green with gardens. The streets of Camelot should be bright with knights and their ladies. Let there be trees everywhere, like green flags set on silver staffs. Camelot! I see a place of gold and stone and marble. A castle of orange and brown and yellow and warm white. A palace where every corner stone and every twig is printed sharply on the sky, whatever the sky.'

Arthur believes in architecture.

He sets to work.

33

Arthur is tall above the ordinary.

His face is sunburnt to a hue nearly as dark as his light bronze hair.

His eyes show clearly bright and pale in contrast.

In his ears hang long pearl and gold ornaments that touch his shoulders.

His tunic is of fine violet silk and embroidered leather.

He carries in his belt a curved knife.

Against his hip he holds a purple cap ornamented with a plume of peacock's feathers.

He wears long gloves which get fretted in the palm with the use of rein and sword.

But more than these details, brothers mine, it is King Arthur's face that strikes the novice.

A face like one of the masks of God.

You heard.

34

Camelot is built and Arthur holds court royal in it.

(O yes, he bored me, little pig.)

To Camelot comes the young wife of the King of Orkney.

Morgan le Fay.

Her eyes like deep pools in a dark wood.

Her hair and eyebrows like the sloe for blackness.

And on her cheeks the redness of poppies.

Morgan.

Her steps are tiny and measured in the manner of Egyptian ladies, and the gems of her slippers make aureoles about her feet.

Her bare arms covered with bracelets the shape of dragons and snakes and worms swallowing their own tails.

Her breasts, full-blown for one so young, encased in two golden bowls. The centres of the bowls surmounted by large rubies.

A sharp nose. Like a vixen's.

Sharp chin.

Black eyes as sharp as knives.

Her teeth, as she smiles, as white as a young animal's.

Morgan.

Morgan le Fay.

The king's half-sister.

35

King Arthur lusts after Morgan le Fay.

I fancy that Morgan uses no more witchcraft in this than a woman usually uses.

The scent of her body.

The rustle of her dress.

The seeming shyness of her little feet going in and out beneath the hem of that dress as she walks and as she dances.

The down of fair hair on the backs of her arms.

The tender white skin at the inside of her elbows.

The charm of the nape of her neck.

The inquisitive angle of her chin.

It is enough, little pig.

Arthur lusts after her.

A young man in his strength, a virgin.

A young woman whose body has presumably been awakened by the attentions of her stepfather, King Lot, but perhaps not satisfied.

Morgan does not seem satisfied.

Her husband is in disgrace because of his rebellion.

Arthur forgives him – every inch the Christian king already – but he will not allow him to show his black beard at court, inside the walls of Camelot.

Only Morgan is permitted that privilege.

'And that,' says Arthur, 'for our mother's sake.'

(He has forgiven his mother her treachery to his father, King Uther Pendragon. As for little Morgan's act of treachery – the sword thrust in the stone, the murder of Igrayne by diabolism . . . My brothers, I am the only one who knows of it. And how do I know? By a picture seen in my head. Once, when I was young, I believed those pictures utterly. It is a curious thing but as I grow older I have less confidence in confiding my visions to another living soul. Perhaps I trust them less myself also? I am one who has seen chance words of fantasy, the seeds of the imagination, translated into fact, grown into furious actuality. I bite my tongue. I say nothing.)

I watch Morgan in the dance in the candlelight.

I watch Arthur watching her also.

Her dress makes a teasing sound as she dances close by him.

Without doubt now I know it.

The girl has been aroused to fleshy pleasures by her stepfather, but comes here now to Camelot unsatisfied.

She gives off that scent. That musk. The enticing, enchanting, and maddening aroma of a young girl worked-up but not brought to the peace of her fulfilment.

I notice it.

Arthur sniffs it out of the smoky air at every corner where she stands or where she dances.

And Morgan le Fay dances a lot. Her body seems only at peace with itself when she is dancing.

Arthur translates his longing into love.

'Merlin,' he says. 'I love her.'

I bite my tongue.

I say nothing.

'I must have her.'

It is the voice of Uther Pendragon all over again. Just so, I sat in this hall, and a woman was dancing, and a king observed her in the candlelight. But that woman was this woman's mother, and this man's mother also . . .

'She is your half-sister,' I tell Arthur. 'It is forbidden.'

'The daughters of Adam and Eve, our first parents, were the wives of Cain and Abel, their brothers.'

'It is a sin, my lord.'

Arthur smiles. His hand plays in the plume of peacock's feathers in his cap. The cap rests on his thigh. 'In Egypt, so I have heard, they say it is sacrilege for a king *not* to marry his sister.'

Morgan's silk gown is blown against her body by a sudden whim of the summer wind.

'You should have something done about the draughts,' I tell the king. 'Camelot may be a castle built to music, but it's absurdly draughty, even on a midsummer's eve . . .'

Arthur ignores my attempt to change the subject. Once he would have joined in the joke, thrown back his head, and laughed. Now his eyes feast hungrily on what the breeze is doing to Morgan's dress – the way it presses the silk against her breasts, and down into the mystery between her legs. He is fascinated. He cannot take his gaze from her.

'Merlin,' he whispers.

'My lord?'

'I wish to see her undressed ...'

'To see the naked body of your half-sister?'

I bite my tongue.

For I know the moment I have uttered them that these words – *To see the naked body of your half-sister?* – have had exactly the same effect on Arthur as some words of mine – *To keep his wife in order?* – once had upon King Uther Pendragon, his father.

My remark inflames the imagination of the king.

From that moment all is lost.

Camelot might as well be a heap of rubble.

The throne of Britain a nest for rats.

'To see the naked body of my half-sister ... Yes!'

I sigh.

'Such things are against law and custom,' I say.

'Then law and custom do not go deep enough into what makes us men.'

'No doubt, but – '

'I tell you, Merlin, *I want to see her naked body!'*

'My lord ...'

'Arrange it for me!'

'I?'

'You! You are good at such things, I fancy? They catch your interest? They amuse you?'

The young king's words alarm me. Their truth catches me by the throat, my brothers. Not that *amuse* is right. *Amuse* misses the horror of the fascination of it altogether.

'My lord king,' I say matter-of-factly, 'there is one way ...'

'Yes?'

'You could question her.'

'*Question* her?'

'She is the wife of a traitor,' I point out. 'You would be quite entitled to put her to the question. Not to make love to her, mind. But to put her to the question.'

'The rack?'

'If you like. But there are subtler instruments, and all of them involve her nakedness.'

King Arthur's hand is shaking as it plays among the peacock feathers.

Now he plucks one out.

'Excellent!' he cries. 'Have the Lady Morgan le Fay brought tonight before me in the secret chamber!'

36

'Merlin, Merlin, am I dreaming?'

'If it is a dream, my lord king, then it is a dream that I share with you.'

'She comes. Morgan le Fay. Little Morgan. My half-sister. She comes before me in the red-draped chamber.'

'Her hair is black, my lord, and her flesh white.'

'Yes! Yes!'

'You question her reasonably.'

'Reasonably, yes.'

'She does not answer.'

'Stubborn girl.'

'She is stubborn, yes, and proud, and defiant, my lord. She thinks you cannot break her silence. Nothing that you say can shake her. You catch her hands. You entreat her on your bended knees. The tears pour down your face. You explain that you do not *want* to hurt her.'

'Do not *want* to hurt her!'

'She still says nothing. Tosses her stubborn head. Stings your face with her hair as she tosses it. You forgive her.'

'Forgive her, yes – '

'But she is careless of your forgiveness also. Her eyes are laughing at you. Darkly bright.'

'Darkly bright eyes – '

'You take her on your lap, my lord king. One arm around her waist. Your other hand – '

'My other hand – '

'Caresses her swelling breasts through the silk stuff of her gown.'

'Yes! Yes!'

'And again you ask her reasonably what you wish to know. But again she says nothing. She does not respond or reply. But her body responds to you. Her body replies. For you can feel beneath the silk her nipples hardening. Lot touched those nipples. Lot sucks them – '

'Her stepfather!'

'Her husband, my lord. The man who has half-awoken this deeply desirable body.'

'Deeply desirable, yes! Ah!'

'Half-awoken but never quite satisfied her.'

'Of course not. He cannot.'

'But you can.'

'Because she wants me. She wants me. She longs for me. *This* is what she dreams of. Me, me.'

'But she slaps your hand away, my lord.'

'She is too modest!'

'Her nipples say yes, but her hand says no.'

'Perhaps she is fearful? *Incest?*'

'I do not think the sin of incest would much deter the Lady Morgan, my lord. Indeed, I think that the fact that to come to your bed would be incest – '

'Excites her? Intrigues her?'

'Who knows what excites and intrigues the Lady Morgan le Fay?'

'Merlin, you blackest of magicians, let us find out! The rack . . .'

'You are importunate, my lord. First, let us undress her.'

'Strip her, yes. Merlin, you have my permission. You understand? It is my will: Remove her gown!'

'I have removed it, my lord. There do you see?'

'My head! I cannot –'

'*The naked body of your half-sister!* The breasts! The thighs!'

'Ah! Ah!'

'Her hair pours down but can't conceal those lovely breasts, my lord. Her little hands – '

'Yes? What are they doing, Merlin?'

'Her little hands are cupped across her sex, to shield it. Like the exquisite shell upon some creature of the ocean floor. The colour of coral.'

'Make her remove her hands, Merlin! I want to – '

'*See*, my lord king? There! You shall see! Now? Do you *see*, now? See the dark triangle of hair, the sweetly swelling mons, the lovely sex of your sister?'

'Morgan! Morgan le Fay! I – '

'Question her, my lord.'

'What?'

'You wish to question her, my lord. It is the purpose. The reason. That is why she has been brought here before you. Tonight. To this secret chamber.'

'Question the wanton? When she looks at me like that! I tell you, Merlin, there is only one question I want to ask her ... Only one thing I want to question her with ...'

'The fasces, my lord?'

'The *what*?'

'The fasces of power. The rods of your authority. Don't you want to whip her with them? Whip the bare buttocks of your wanton sister?'

'I do! Yes! I do!'

'Then so you shall, my lord, for here they are. Look! Delivered into your hand! The wands of power! Now, now, lay on!'

'You hold her for me, Merlin!'

'I am holding her, my lord.'

'Her head down – '

'Her head is down, my lord – '

'Between your legs – '

'The Lady Morgan's head is between my legs, my lord king.'

'Get out your member, Merlin!'

'My lord?'

'Your prick, man! Quick! Make her suck it! Make my sister take you in her mouth while I whip her bottom! I want to see that! I want to see her sucking you! I want – '

'. . .?'

'. . .!'

'. . .??'

'. . .!!'

'My lord king, you have whipped her enough!'

'No I haven't! No, I haven't!'

'My lord! Her back!'

'She deserves this! She – '

'The branding iron, my lord.'

'Merlin!'

'The iron!'

'It is hot enough?'

'It is just right, my lord. So! She shall bear your brand for ever! Morgan le Fay! There, there, upon the sweetest, the tenderest, the most kissable part of the thigh. The letter A.'

'Merlin! My head!'

'The question . . .'

'I – '

'You must *question* her, my lord king. It is what she is here for. Little Morgan. Your sister. In this secret chamber.'

'The question. Ah! Yes! Merlin, shall we rack her now? Shall we see my sister's body on the rack? Shall we? Shall we?'

'You are importunate, my lord. There are one or two other little things we might do to her before we come to the rack . . .'

37

'And in the morning,' says the devil my father, 'Sir Perceval arose, and when he went forth, behold a shower of snow had fallen the night before, and a hawk had killed a wild fowl in front of the hermit's cell. And the noise of Sir Perceval's horse scared the hawk away, and a raven alighted upon the bird. And Sir Perceval stood, and compared the blackness of the raven and the whiteness of the snow and the redness of the blood to the hair of the lady that he loved best, which was blacker than jet, and to her skin, which was whiter than the snow, and to the two red spots upon her cheeks, which were redder than the blood upon the snow.'

38

'And Sir Perceval grinned,' say my uncle Astarot and my uncle Beelzebub together, 'Sir Perceval grinned like a fox eating shit out of a wire brush.'

39

'Merlin, Merlin, am I dreaming?'

'If it is a dream, my lord king, then it is a dream that I share with you . . .'

O brothers mine, it *is* a dream.

I think . . .

Or, rather, shall we say, a drug-induced hallucination?

I am giving the drug to Arthur (unknown to him) to stanch his passion. To deflect him from his course of ruin. To prevent his incest with the Lady Morgan.

And, yes, little pig, it is a dream that I share with him.

Merlin the dream maker.

I eat the red-and-white capped mushroom too.

Fly-agaric.

Oh, it is in one of these dreams that Arthur dreams of the Questing Beast. In the dream he has been hunting, and lies down to rest by a river. There is a great noise through the woods, as of many hounds barking in pursuit of the stag. Then a long beast comes into the clearing, and drinks from the river thirstily. And the noise of the hounds is the noise which the Questing Beast makes in its throat.

Question. When the Questing Beast drank from the river, did it make a noise in its throat like the barking of many hounds drowning?

Old fool!

My original country was the region of the summer stars.

I journey with the king in his imagination.

I feed him with the mushroom, the sacred diet.

A diet of death.

A secret diet. (He has no idea.)

These red and white caps of magic burn certain odd-angled holes in your brain, dear darling daughter, and *through* the holes men see heaven and hell, paradise and the quality of the inferno.

I feast upon the mushrooms in my crystal cave.

The green walls are covered with them, they grow like lichen, they are the spore of rain and moonlight.

So –

King Arthur dreams.

King Arthur dreams of what he would like to do.

King Arthur dreams of what he would like to do to his half-sister, Queen Morgan le Fay. In his darkened and most secret red-draped heart.

And I provide for him.

Merlin the feeder of the king's imagination.

Merlin the companion in hell.

Merlin the sharer of the dream.

Or so I think . . .

How they must be laughing at me, my father the Emperor Lucifer and his dark lieutenants!

For we give rein now to every impulse of Arthur's. I conjure up Queen Morgan in accordance with any wild wish that occurs to him.

A fancy crosses his mind, and I see to it that it is performed.

King Arthur enjoys the body of his half-sister in a dozen wicked ways.

He frigs her.

He fucks her.

He sucks her.

He buggers her.

The whip, the scourge, the birch, the horsewhip.

The rack and the whipping post.

Every night for a month there is some new twist of ingenuity to the king's pleasure in that white and wanton body.

By night.

Always by night.

In the king's bed chamber.

And in the secret red-draped chamber far beneath the castle of Camelot.

Where, by day, and on the ground level, there is no one gentler than Arthur, no knight or baron more kind and courteous, more shiveringly chivalrous, and none so quick to come to the defending of a maiden's honour.

Camelot the golden.

Built upon a secret cesspool.

A very perfect gentle knight.

Who likes to whip girls' bottoms.

A noble king. The noblest.

Revelling in incest with his sister.

I, Merlin, alone, know the truth about all this.

Or *think* I know the truth ...

O Christ, how they must laugh at me!

For the truth is, in fact, more complicated and more real than I imagine.

And I, the trickster, have been tricked ...

For behold, there comes the night when I have fed the king *no* mushrooms, and the red-and-white capped drug has no hold on him, nor on me, and I have made no invocations to call up the phantom of Queen Morgan for his imaginary pleasures, yet the door of the secret red-draped chamber opens and she comes in to us, Morgan le Fay, with her black hair like the raven's wing and her skin that is whiter than snow.

And she curtsies mockingly before me –

'My lord Merlin!' –

Before lifting her dress shamelessly before the king her brother, and saying:

'What is your pleasure tonight, my dear?'

It is the *real* Morgan, O Jesukin.

No phantom. No drug-conjured ghost. No eidolon.

The real Morgan le Fay. His flesh-and-blood half-sister,

spawn of the Lady Igrayne and the dark Duke of Cornwall, wife of her own stepfather, King Lot of Orkney.

Lifting her black-as-hell gown.

'My lord Merlin, do not avert your eyes,' the witch says wantonly. 'I show you nothing you have not seen – and touched – a dozen times. Yes, touched – even you, the eunuch for the sake of the kingdom of . . . what? Heaven? hell? or your own fearful heart?'

King Arthur is amused. The idiot.

He reaches for her.

For his half-sister, Queen Morgan le Fay.

He kisses her.

His hand plays in her dress.

In her lap.

She laughs.

She wriggles.

She kicks her legs.

White legs kicking.

And Morgan le Fay laughing at me where I stare at her in disbelief.

'Yes, my lord Merlin! Oh yes, it is real! It is real! And I am real! Here, here, upon – what was it? – ah yes! – how could I forget? – here, here, upon the sweetest, the tenderest, the most kissable part of the thigh . . .'

The letter A.

40

Arthur has dreamt again of the Questing Beast.

(It is a symptom of withdrawal from the drug.)

Now he wakes and wanders in the wood.

Little wolf, my brother, he is full of remorse. His incest with Morgan le Fang hangs heavily upon his conscience. He walks with me in agony through the castle, pestering himself, tugging at my sleeve. *'What did I do? What did you make me do?'* In truth, I *made* the king do nothing. I fulfilled his fantasies, as I thought, fictitiously, and with phantoms. But Morgan and my father the devil outwitted us, so it seems. The brand of the king on her thigh is a real brand. That is unarguable. And the child that will kick soon in her womb is a real child.

Mordred.

Bastard son of King Arthur and his half-sister.

Fruit of incest.

Destroyer of the Round Table.

Queen Morgan has been sent back to King Lot.

She will bear her child in Orkney, and no one will know that King Lot is not the father of it.

Him.

Mordred.

That black and hump-backed lump of incest.

The truth about Camelot.

The truth about King Arthur.

Mordred.

Mordred is the truth about King Arthur.

My sorrow, my sweetness, do I go too quickly for you?

Forgive me. Past and future are as one to me.

I am a man shut in the present tense.

I see King Arthur wandering in the wood. I could as easily see Mordred dead, and looking for his head, wandering towards the king through the trees after the last battle. I mean: in the same moment. I am told that different time scales are involved. Arthur howling in the green wood with remorse was *then*. The last battle is *to come*. In Merlin's head there is neither *then* nor *to come*. All, all is present to me, equally.

Arthur rides on.

The king rides fiercely.

His horse's flanks are bloody from his spurs.

Great cruel spurs.

(I always hated them.)

In days of old, when knights were trivial.

So –

King Arthur comes to a rich pavilion, which has been set beside the high road, by a well of fresh water.

And there sits a knight upon his war-horse. A knight in green armour.

'Sir knight!' cries Arthur. 'Out of my way!'

'It is my custom to stand here,' the knight says.

'I will make you change it,' Arthur says.

'And I will defend my custom,' says the knight.

Then they draw apart, and come together riding at full tilt.

They meet.

Hard.

So hard that both spears shiver into little pieces as each hits the centre of the other's shield.

King Arthur goes to draw his sword.

But the Green Knight says:

'Not so. Let us run together with spears again.'

'I would,' Arthur says. 'If I had another spear . . .'

'I have spears,' says the Green Knight.

He instructs his squire to bring two from the pavilion.

Now once again the two men joust together – King Arthur and the Green Knight. And once again their spears break into fragments without either of them being struck from his horse.

A third time.

This time Arthur's spear breaks again, but the Green Knight's spear does not. Arthur is knocked to the ground.

Now Arthur springs to his feet in a great fury.

He draws his sword and shouts defiance at the Green Knight.

The Green Knight comes down from his horse. He draws his own sword.

A terrible battle of swords begins. They hack at each other. They hew. They swing. They cut pieces off each other's shields and armour. Each of them suffers so many wounds that the trampled grass in front of the pavilion is stained red with their blood. Just once they rest. Then they rush together again. And this time Arthur's sword is broken in half. He is left with the useless hilt in his bare hand.

'Will you yield?' says the Green Knight laconically.

'Death is more welcome,' says bold King Arthur.

And, so saying, he leaps in under the Green Knight's sword, and seizes him round the waist and hurls him headlong to the ground.

They roll together.

First Arthur is uppermost, and then the Green Knight.

But the Green Knight is still the stronger, and in a little while he tears off Arthur's helmet and snatches again at his sword to cut the king's head off.

I fall as a dewdrop from the trees above them, becoming myself before I touch the ground.

I tap the Green Knight on the shoulder.

'Sir knight,' I say. 'Hold your hand! If you strike this stroke then Logres dies and Camelot is no longer. If you strike this stroke then Britain will be a waste land.'

'It *is* a waste land,' says the Green Knight. Then he peers closely at his victim.

'Who is it?' he demands.

'It is King Arthur!' I tell him.

The Green Knight throws his sword into a tree.

He throws it with such force and accuracy that it goes deep into the trunk, and stays there, twanging.

'King Arthur,' the Green Knight says.

He spits in Arthur's face.

Then he sinks back against the tree beside the well of clear water, and falls into a deep sleep.

I help the king to mount his horse.

He is sore wounded.

I lead him away through the forest.

Arthur is twisted with pain and shame and guilt.

Merlin, Merlin, what have I done? Why did that knight spit in my face when he heard my name? What does it mean? What does it signify? Does everyone now despise me? Do they *know*? Must my sins be common knowledge? Tell me, should I not have had Queen Morgan put to death? Before the child is born? Should I not – '

'The child will be born,' I tell him. 'Its name will be Mordred. It will lead the army that will fight you in the last battle.'

'The last battle? You mean I shall lose it?'

I shrug. 'Every battle is lost *and* won,' I say. 'You will not lose it, but you will not win it either. You will not die afterwards, but you will no longer be among the living.'

'And Mordred?'

I gesture around us at the forest.

'He will be here. He will be dead and looking for his head among the acorns.'

I bring King Arthur to a cave.

I dress his wounds. I bind them up with herbs.

In three days he is whole again.

His mind, however, is still distraught.

'I have no sword,' he says.

It is his one complaint. Night and day. He laments his swordlessness.

'Your sword is waiting for you,' I tell him. 'Come.'

We ride again into the forest. Deeper. Deeper. Deeper than any man has ever been.

We come at last to a lake which is the colour of steel made blue by fire.

'See!'

In the very centre of the lake, in the middle of the blue circle which it makes in the dark forest, there is an arm upstretched and holding a sword. The arm is clothed in white samite. The sword is beautiful. The sword has a golden hilt all studded with jewels, and a jewelled scabbard and belt also.

'The sword Excalibur!' I tell him.

Then Arthur sees a woman dressed in pale blue silk with a golden girdle. The woman is walking across the water towards him. Presently she stands before us on the shore.

'I am the Lady of the Lake,' she says. 'The sword Excalibur awaits you there. Do you wish to take the sword and wear it at your side?'

'Lady,' meek King Arthur says, 'I am not worthy.'

'Then you are worthy,' says the woman. 'Enter this boat now ...'

There is a barge upon the water.

Arthur steps into the barge.

The Lady of the Lake stands on the shore behind him, and the barge moves through the blue water as if her thoughts are drawing it by the keel.

It moves on, the barge, black through blue, until Arthur comes beside the arm clothed in white samite.

Leaning from the barge, he takes the sword Excalibur and the scabbard.

At once the arm and the hand sink down out of sight beneath the waters.

King Arthur comes back to the shore of the lake.

The Lady is gone also.

King Arthur ties the barge to the roots of a tree.

He comes up towards me from the water, buckling the sword Excalibur to his side as he comes.

'Which do you like better, the sword or the scabbard?' I ask him.

'The sword, silly!'

'Then you have all to learn yet,' I tell him. 'The scabbard is worth ten such swords.'

The Gold Book

1

The white hart runs in, and the brachet runs after it.

The knights wait by torchlight in the great hall of Camelot.

King Arthur and his knights.

King Arthur and his queen.

Little pig, I have promised them miracles.

And the white hart runs in, and the brachet runs after it, and behind the white brachet a pack of sixty great black hounds all baying their heads off.

We are at the wedding of King Arthur and Guinevere.

Guinevere, Queen Guinevere, Gug-gug-gug-gug-Guinevere, only daughter of King Leodegraunce of Camelerde. King Arthur first met her at the siege of Scapa Flow when her father waged war on King Lot of Orkney, and won back the Round Table which was given away, to the kingdom's downfall, by the Lady Igrayne.

Now Lot lies dead in a shallow water grave, and fishes feast on him.

There are minnows in his skull.

Morgan le Fay has fled, and her son Mordred with her.

'I hope to Christ the devil's spawn are dead!' says Arthur of his sister and his son.

I know that they are not.

(They are in fact at Mons Badonicus, in sanctuary at the convent of the Flaming Heart.)

King Arthur tells me also of his love for the rare Guinevere:

'Merlin, I adore her. Merlin, I will marry her. There is an illumination about her. Merlin, this is quite different from the lust I felt for Morgan.'

'Quite different?'

'A different world.'

I bite my tongue then. As per usual.

I say nothing.

The Round Table is borne back to Camelot on an iron cart by a knight of Camelerde. This knight's name is Lancelot. Lancelot is tall and quick and magnificently whiskered. He pulls the iron cart with six black horses, riding one of them himself and sporting a silver helmet. He brings the Lady Guinevere with him also. She rides in a pearl-encrusted litter, with red velvet cushions and curtains of samite silk. Lancelot is her escort, her equerry, the captain of her bodyguard. Leodegraunce esteems the bright knight as a son. The Round Table is being returned to Camelot as the young bride's dowry. O little pig, as they ride under the flag-draped arch over Watling Street and into Logres I see the way that Lancelot looks at Guinevere, and Guinevere looks at Lancelot. Those looks are not quite different. Those looks do not belong to another world.

King Arthur marries Guinevere at Pentecost.

Two fat archbishops join their hands.

Four knights bear the golden swords in front of them as they come down the porphyry stair of Saint Paul's.

One of these knights: the same Sir Lancelot.

Lancelot, Lancelot, what a big moustache you've got.

2

'Yup,' says my uncle A, sitting like a cormorant on the top branch of the Tree of Life. 'Hear all we angels, progeny of light, thrones, dominations, princedoms, virtues, powers. I told you they call me Fuckalot in the second circle.'

He shits diminished stars.

'This Lance has been tickling Guggy's fancy all along,' he confides. 'He had his moustache into her twat before she knew what it was for. It's where her stammer comes from, so Freud says.'

My uncle Beelzebub gives a miserable smile.

'I have noticed,' he says, 'that the same thing goes on happening all the time. First it was the ever so virgin Vivien and the cosmocrator. Then it was Igrayne and King Uther Pendragon. Then it was Morgan le Fay and wet King Arthur. And now, no doubt – '

'Everybody's doing it, doing it, doing it. Pick your nose and chewing it, chewing it, chewing it,' Astarot sings. 'There is one story and one story only,' he adds solemnly.

'Of course,' says my father the devil. 'It is *his* story.'

'His?'

'Merlin's.'

My father sits in darkness, hatching things.

'It *was* not his story,' he goes on. 'Not at the start. He was Merlin the watcher, Merlin the magician, Merlin the unmoved mover. In his inviolability. His virginity.'

He giggles, my daddy.

'We'll soon change that now,' he promises.

Astarot wipes his bottom on an apostate.

'You didn't do too well with little Morgan,' the count says critically. 'And she was being hailed as a perfect specimen, as I recall.'

'Book 3, chapter 20,' Beelzebub confirms, looking.

The Emperor Lucifer shrugs his heron's shoulders. 'I didn't do too badly either,' he protests. 'I made Merlin think that he could make a fool of me. (Red and white mushrooms indeed!) *And* I got quite a stimulating whipping into the bargain.' He rubs his crescent buttocks thoughtfully. 'What that failed Antichrist underestimates all the time is the extent to which I make *him* also. What we are approaching now, my dears, is the moment when Merlin the so-called maker is unmade.'

'When we reach it,' Astarot asks, 'can I tell you about the Sleeve Job?'

'There's a time and a place for everything,' says my father.

3

The white hart runs in, and the brachet runs after it.

Gug-gug-gug-gug-Guinevere.

She was a stammerer, Queen Guinevere the golden, one of

those charmingly fickle ladies who take their own mood from whatever male company they are keeping, quick-tempered, sweet, obliging, but needing distractions, and riding on the cheering crowds like a very nervous surfer on a wave.

Queen Guinevere, that great queen, mistress of Logres, first lady of Camelot.

That great bitch, mistress of Lancelot, first lady to take off her knickers when the king's back was turned.

I mean: Guinevere couldn't wait for Arthur to be off and about some Quest or another and she'd be straight down the corridor and into Sir Lancelot's bed. The king's love for her might belong to a different world, but it was not a world that interested her. What interested her was the lance between Lancelot's legs. And sometimes his moustaches.

O yes, I saw them, dear darling daughter.

I watched them at it, brother wolf.

As lovers, they were not original.

(With one exception, which I will be coming to.)

Their antics, by and large, are scarcely worth recording.

Suffice to say that they started anew the night of the royal wedding.

My brothers, it is true.

Guinevere lay bored and golden from her husband's respectful caresses.

King Arthur stepped outside for a necessary purpose.

And out pops Sir Lancelot from the bedroom cupboard, wax on his moustaches and his lance at the ready.

He's finished and away down the back stairs, by the time the fastidious king returns.

'Good night, my dear.'

'Good night, sweet dreams, good night.'

'*A different world, Merlin.*'

Queen Guinevere, that great bitch.

Gug-gug-gug-gug-Guinevere.

A miracle of rose and thorn, my brothers.

She talked in her bath too, enjoying the echoes. Arthur's steward, Sir Kay, thought that there must be two or three people in there with her in the tub full of unicorn milk. Sometimes there were (Gug-Gug and Lancelot, or Gug-Gug and half a dozen other knights without their armour on), but often it was just the queen titillating and seducing herself in different voices.

The queen of love and beauty, fanned by ladies in red.

Red shoes too, if you want to know. Guinevere liked to be attended in the bath by ladies of the bedchamber in red shoes.

Don't ask me why, brother wolf.

Queen Guggy's hair was brown.

Gold-shot, as she said.

Gold-shot, but not of its own virtue.

In and out of it she wore threaded a fine gold chain.

Behind, it was plaited in a long twist.

Plaited and bound up in cloth of gold till it looked as hard and tight as a bull's tail.

Her favourite question:

'Whah-whah-what did *you* have for breakfast?'

Guinevere's dress.

Queen Guinevere's dress was usually of formal brocade, green and white, or gold and white, and falling to her feet.

It was cut square at the neck.

And from that square her throat, dazzling white, shot up as stiff as a stalk which should find in her face its delicate flower.

She was not very rosy, save about the lips.

Guinevere's eyes.

Queen Guinevere's eyes were grey, inclined to be green, the lashes black.

'Whah-whah-what did *you* have for breakfast?'

As for her shape.

Sumptuous as the proud queen's dress was.

Stiff and straight and severe.

I ask you, Jesus, to believe, my pig, that she had grace to fill her dress with life.

To move at ease in it.

To press it into soft and rounded lines.

There were, however, problems.

One day a cow came and poked its head through the window of the nice room King Arthur had built on to Camelot for the queen to do her adultery in. Guinevere laughed but she was upset. Arthur had the solution. He flooded the field and drowned the cow.

4

'Let's have a turn-turn-turna-tournament,' says Queen Guinevere.

This was to celebrate the wedding.

And so we had a tournament, my brothers.

(Arthur did everything Guinevere told him:

The once and future husband.)

It was Arthur and his party, in white, against Lancelot and his party, in black.

Lancelot had three knights only, on his side.

All in black from head to foot, black visors down so that you could not see their faces, and on their shields a strange device:

A worm that swallowed its own tail.

These three, with Sir Lancelot, put down Sir Acolon, Sir Ballamore, Sir Beaumaris, Sir Beleobus, Sir Belvoure, Sir Bersunt, Sir Bors, Sir Eric, Sir Ewain, Sir Floll, Sir Gaheris, Sir Galahad, Sir Galohalt, Sir Gareth, Sir Gauriel, Sir Grislet, Sir Kay, Sir Lamerock, Sir Lionell, Sir Marhaus, Sir Palamide, Sir Pauqinet, Sir Pelleas, Sir Sagris, Sir Superabilis, Sir Tristan de Leonnais, Sir Turquine, Sir Wigalois, and Sir Wigamur.

Thirty knights (if you count King Arthur) defeated by three plus Sir Lancelot du Lac.

When the tournament was done, the trysting ground was littered with knights with cracked heads and knights with carved bodies, knights with their shields and their hauberks in rags, knights who could hardly see between the bars of their visors for the sweat and the blood in their eyes. Knights stuck upside-down in holes in the ground, where great blows had hammered them like so many tent pegs. Knights tied back to back in their own tackle. Knights minus right legs. Knights minus left legs. Knights minus legs altogether.

The white party thus.

The black party riding in triumph to the pavilion where

Queen Guinevere sat applauding them softly. Pale hands. Clap. Clap.

Beyond her gold head: Camelot. Its towers as white as snow, its long banners, its battlements awash with sun through fog, the shields of many colours on its gates.

Lancelot bows low in the saddle.

The queen tosses him a pair of her golden panties.

Lancelot raises them high on his lance.

His moustache springs out – ping! – on either side of his smile.

Vast applause from the crowd.

The black knights do a lap of honour.

5

Three knights in black.

I smell the breath of one of them as he trots past.

The second is surrounded by a cloud of flies.

The third has an eye looking out of the top of his helmet.

6

After the tournament.

Guinevere and Lancelot in the rose garden.

His black horse tethered at the gate to the garden. Its flanks sweat-lathered, blood-flecked, dripping.

Lancelot stands among the falling petals.

The queen takes his prick out.

She kneels before him in the garden.

She unpicks her champion's armour between the legs and takes out Lancelot's prick. The sinful queen.

She rubs his prick in her hair.

Gug-gug-gug-gug-Guinevere.

Golden hair.

The hard bull's pizzle of her plaits unplucked.

Queen Guinevere masturbating the king's friend Sir Lancelot

du Lac in her soft and gold-shot hair, holding him through her tresses, tossing him off as he stands before her, his puissance, his seed jetting among the rose petals, staining the red ones white.

The singing of the birds and the shining of the sun.

I watch in the shape of a sundial.

Merlin the sun's dark hand.

7

After the tournament.

Guinevere and Arthur on the Round Table.

The king in despair at his defeat in the jousting.

Determined to put a brave face upon it.

He comes to the queen.

Guinevere in a blue silk dress.

Arthur and Guinevere alone in the great hall of Camelot.

(Alone? You're never alone with a magician. I watch them. Merlin the Siege Perilous.)

Arthur persuades his wife to lie down on her back on the Round Table.

He has her blue silk dress up.

But his once and future prick's not up.

Won't.

Can't.

Arthur is impotent. A Fisher King without a rod. His incest with Queen Morgan has unmanned him. He lives at the centre of a homo-erotic web of knights, and Queen Guinevere is free to pursue her lust with his best friend, the ultra-knightly Lancelot.

O scarlet-capped Lancelot.

Feathered, slashed, and booted Lancelot.

Slightly bow-legged Lancelot, who keeps the ends of his moustache tucked in his boots.

Fucking Guinevere on the Round Table, Arthur is trying to fuck Lancelot and all his knights.

But he can't.

Won't.

Cannot.
The once and future orgasm is beyond him.
With man or woman, knight or lady.
The act of love is evil to King Arthur now.
The act of love means Morgan le Fay.
The letter A.
The brand on her thigh. The whip across her bottom.
Mordred, son of incest.
Mordred, the woodworm in the Round Table.
Mordred, the death of Arthur.
Queen Guinevere laughing at her husband's efforts.
'Another defeat for the why-why-why-why-white knight, my lord?'

8

Watching Guinevere and Lancelot, watching Guinevere and Arthur – I despair.
The tears run down my face, my Jesukin.
I weep. I rage.
(Dew on the sundial, yes. And a pool like dog's piss under the Siege Perilous.)
My father is right.
The world is a book.
And the devil writes it.

9

Now the white hart runs in.
And the brachet runs after it.
And behind the white brachet a pack of sixty great black hounds.
Howling their heads off.
Round the Round Table runs the white hart.
Round the Round Table runs the white brachet.
Round the Round Table run the sixty black hounds.

A snake or a worm swallowing its own tail.
Making a noise like the Questing Beast.
And Arthur is saying:
'What does it *mean*? What does it *signify*?'
And Guinevere is saying:
'Whah-whah-what did *you* have for breakfast?'
But Lancelot is saying nothing. He is stroking his moustaches.

Round the Round Table run hart, black hounds, and brachet, and as the uroborus of it streams towards the door again, the great gold door of Camelot, up jumps the brachet and leaps against the hart's flank snapping and yapping, so that the white hart lunges desperately, crazily, and stumbles, to one side, to the left, knocking over Lancelot where he's curling his whisker ends.

Lancelot knocked from his chair.
Lancelot down on the floor.
The brachet straddles him.
The brachet sniffs at the fallen knight.
It cocks its leg against him.

Up leaps Sir Lancelot with a roar, his nose bleeding all down his moustaches, drip, drip, and he seizes the brachet by the tail.

He seizes the brachet and he strides out of the hall.
Swinging the brachet round his head.
He jumps upon his stallion and he spurs it away.
With the brachet still squealing under his arm.

O and the black hounds bell away into the forest after the white hart, but before the bell of their baying has died into the distance, comes riding into the great gold hall of Camelot –

You.
You.
You.
In the form of a damsel on a white palfrey.

There is a green leaf in your hair. A green leaf caught in all that gold.

Hair more gold than the flowers of the broom.
Hands more white than the foam of the wave.
Cheeks as red as the foxgloves of the moor.
You step from your steed.

(Click of your shoes! Green leaf in your golden hair!)

You come walking before King Arthur.

'My lord king,' you say. 'That brachet is mine which your false knight has stolen.'

'It's no affair of ours!' King Arthur says.

'Boo hoo!' says Gug-gug-Guinevere. 'But I want Lancelot back!'

10

'Where's Astarot?' says my uncle B suspiciously.

My daddy makes a proud shape with his blasting rod. 'Three guesses,' he offers. Then, as his grand treasurer frowns and grins, he adds: 'Book 1, chapter 40 . . . Remember where he said he'd been while we endured the childbirth and the monk's fall from the tower?'

Beelzebub strokes a fly with relish. His blue face shines.

'Up Guinevere's,' he says.

The devil pops a violet in his mouth. 'Right,' he says. 'You're not so insectiferous as you look.'

'I get the drift,' says uncle B. 'Astarot inhabits our knight of the vast moustaches.'

'For the time being,' says my daddy. 'Fuckalot Lancelot. The shape suits him, eh?'

Beelzebub considers the toes of his ginger boots. 'Don't tell me,' he says gloomily. 'You have a role for me too, cosmocrator?'

'Yes, I have.'

'Friar Blaise I hated. What a part that was for a prince of hell!'

'I think you'll like this better. It's not hard. Not too demanding, Beelzie. In fact, the easiest of the lot.'

My uncle B looks up and groans.

'King Arthur?'

'Right on!'

'King creepy Arthur?'

'Don't echo my son's cynicisms.'

'Arthur, Arthur, don't know whether to call you Martha.' My uncle B shakes his long thin head. 'The once and future cretin does your will more or less without my help.'

'So far, so bad,' admits the devil. 'But he's not too bright at being dark, and we're going to need you now. The plot thickens.'

'The plot? What plot?'

'Ah, ah, my doctor of the diptera, you do not pay attention. Cast your mind back to the end of Book 2. The White Book. Merlin as Nineve trotting through the tapestry. Merlin wandering in the painted forest. And what he saw there, and what he heard.'

'I recall all that,' says Beelzebub. 'Uther and Igrayne, of course. The glass wall. What Astarot called the one story and one story only.'

'And the question Merlin heard?'

'What question?'

'Whom does this Grail serve?'

'Oh that,' says Beelzebub dully. 'Yes, I remember it now. And something about a lance and a cup too, wasn't there? But that seemed obscure to me. I couldn't follow – '

'So you said before. Well, soon you will follow. Soon you will have no choice. Soon it will all be as clear as day. Or everlasting night.' Lucifer tunes up his fiddle and plays a quick variation on a theme of Paganini. 'Meretricious,' he says. 'Mind you, that stradivarius has never been quite the same since I hammered it to bits. Now listen, flyblow. Remember what I told you. When Merlin meets the one who watched Igrayne and Uther at their love games, when Merlin loves the one who loved to watch that coupling through the green glass of the forest, then we shall have him, then he will be ours ... And that, ducky, is the moment that approaches now! The dénouement! The end of the Round Table!'

My uncle Beelzebub says:

'But, Emperor, it has hardly begun.'

'The Round Table lasts only as long as Merlin is master of it,' Lucifer replies. 'Once Merlin is undone then the thing is just so much firewood.'

'And Arthur?' says my uncle B.

'Arthur Martha, as you say. The end of Merlin is the start of the *Morte Darthur*.'

My uncle Beelzebub shakes his head doubtfully.

'And how will Merlin be unmade? What do you have in store for him?'

The Emperor Lucifer giggles.

He writhes. He preens himself.

He makes a fan of his fingers and simpers behind it.

He winks the eye in the middle of his forehead.

His fingernails are suddenly bright red.

11

King Arthur is crying, 'Bugger your brachet, madam!' when all at once a bluebottle lands on his nose and crawls up inside his right nostril. He sneezes, but that does not expel the fly. Then he says: 'Saddle my horse! Saddle horses for all of us! We ride to the Quest! This theft of brachets is a terrible thing!'

Queen Guinevere glares at him through her tears.

'It was self-self-self-defence!' she hisses. 'Lancelot did not steal it. The brachet attacked him!'

Her husband placates her:

'This theft of Lancelots is a terrible thing also! We ride to rescue both of them! My horse! My horse!'

We ride away west into the forest of Broceliande. Unpathed, its bright green fathoms. O great sea-rooted wood! Extension of my mind! Dark place of peace!

King Arthur rides first, with Queen Guinevere beside him.

Accompanying the royal couple rides Sir Perceval, a brave and noble youth, the king's chief bodyguard. Perceval is a brilliant boy, dressed all in blue, blue cap, blue cloak, blue breeches, and his boots stained with the summer dust. He sings a carol as he rides: *Bow down you sweet cherry tree.* O yes, I recognize it, little pig. The sweet words echo in the woodlands. The last rays of the sun fall slantwise through tall trees.

We ride behind the royal party, you and I.
You ride on the white palfrey.
I ride on a black mare.
Another knight, Sir Gawain of Verulam, brings up the rear.
Night falls and the forest is now all simultaneity. We journey onwards as if undersea. We ride across a pine-strewn floor of dreams. When it gets dark and darker it seems the fallen cones are stars pricked out in frosty moonlight, so that we ride across the floor of heaven.
But it is very earth. The smell of leaf-mould all around. Our horses' ankles sinking in it. Rustle of leaves. The air heavy with the burden of midsummer.
Far off, and from time to time, we can hear the hounds bell away into the forest after the white hart. And sometimes (perhaps) the thunder of Lancelot's horse.
'Faster! Fast-fast-faster!' cries Queen Guinevere.
Her entreaties grow stronger as the night grows darker.
She stands up in her stirrups and calls out:
'Lancelot!'
The deep woods echo with the single name.
Her gold plait lashes her green-brocaded shoulders as she spurs her horse forward in the moonlight.
King Arthur and Sir Perceval ride away after her.
'Lancelot! My La-la-la-la-Lancelot!'
The last that I hear is the queen's shrill peacock cry.

12

'This is extremely boring,' says my uncle Beelzebub. 'Inhabiting King Arthur is like sitting inside a blancmange. What is the point of it? Where are we going?'
'Towards the end,' says my father. 'Towards the Grail Castle.'
'The Grail?' says uncle B. 'That old pot!' He groans and grins. 'The Holy bloody Grail,' he goes on. 'What I've always wondered is what the hell anyone would ever want to *do* with it once they'd found it!'

My daddy shakes a dreadful dart at him.
'That's blasphemy!' he says.

13

Sir Gawain is getting lost in the forest of Broceliande. He can't keep up with us, any more than we can keep up with Arthur and Guinevere and Perceval, any more than they can catch up with Lancelot and the brachet. And ahead of us all run the white hart and the sixty great black hounds that are howling their heads off.

Sir Gawain is young and handsome and tall and romantic.

He's dressed in a surcoat of satin and a mantle that's trimmed with gold.

When he realizes that he has lost touch with the rest of the Quest he does not panic.

He climbs into a tree to sleep.

He shuts his eyes and pulls his cap over his ears.

In the morning, he thinks, he'll ride along in the forest looking for Quests and adventures all of his own.

14

We are lost too. In another part of the forest.

The trees are very tall and high and growing close together.

There is no moon.

I make a fire and we sit beside it in silence.

I cannot see your face. It is turned towards the dark.

At last you speak:

'Merlin,' you say.

'Yes.'

'Do you know what it is – the esplumoir?'

'A cage,' I say. 'A cage for a moulting hawk.'

'Yes,' you say. 'It is the place of transformations.'

Then you speak again:

'Merlin,' you say.

'Yes.'

'Do you know what it is – the green and burning tree?'

'I have heard of such things,' I say. 'Trees one side flames and the other side green leaves growing.'

You speak a third time:

'Merlin,' you say.

'Yes.'

'Do you know what it is – the crystal cave?'

'Well,' I say. 'A sort of prison, no doubt.'

You laugh then.

Then you turn to me in the firelight.

'Merlin,' you say. 'I have come to take you to your esplumoir, your green and burning tree, your crystal cave. I have come to take you to yourself.'

15

'But she has no face!' protests my uncle Beelzebub. 'Her face is like a looking glass. He is looking at himself!'

My daddy writhes and giggles.

'You get on with your King Arthuring,' he says. 'Astarot has got our knight of the moustaches to the Grail Castle and it's up to you to join him there with Guinevere and Perceval.'

Beelzebub shrugs. He concentrates on the job in hand.

16

And now King Arthur and his queen, accompanied by the faithful knight Sir Perceval, find themselves in a glade of shadows.

The moon rides out from a cloud that is shaped like a dragon.

They see that the glade is oak trees on three sides, including the side through which they have come in entering it. The trees are close together and brimming with owls. There is moon after moon in the eyeballs of the owls.

The fourth side of the glade is a castle of solid glass.

It is the Grail Castle.

A black cock crows.

Even in the darkness Guinevere knows it must be black.

She crosses herself.

A shiver runs down her spine under her gown of green and gold brocade.

'What-whah-what did *you* have for breakfast?' she demands aloud, of no one in particular.

'My lady?' says Sir Perceval, who had porridge.

'Disappointment,' says King Arthur, stepping from his stirrups. 'Horse-flies and disappointment.'

'You,' cries Sir Lancelot, twisting his moustaches into spikes on the topmost tower of the Glass Castle. 'You, you, and blood. And I want you for dinner too.'

'You,' hoot the owls.

'Disappointment,' cry the crickets.

17

Round the Grail Castle runs the white hart.

Round the Grail Castle run the sixty black hounds.

Round the Grail Castle run King Arthur and Queen Guinevere and Sir Perceval.

Then Sir Lancelot opens the door on the moving wheel, and they all run in, white hart and white brachet, black hounds and King Arthur and Queen Guinevere and Sir Perceval of Wales.

18

My uncle B is wrong. You have several faces.

'Who are you?' I say softly.

One moment my mother the virgin Vivien sits by the fire. She nurses me at her breast and sings me to sleep.

Then when I awake the Lady Igrayne is beside me. She runs like a lapwing on tiptoe, but naked, in one silver slipper.

Or else most disturbing of all the little Queen Morgan le Fay, her black-as-hell gown, dancing in the firelight, musky, teasing, her body at peace in the steps of the dance, the letter A burning burning burning on her thigh as she turns to come back to me.

In different shifting forest lights, as the moon shines on you, your hair is black and then golden, your eyes are blue and then green. Sometimes they blaze like the jewels whose names I've forgotten. You change all the time as you move in and out of the shadows.

There is a rose like a red wound between your breasts.

You pluck the rose from your dress and give it to me.

'Nimue,' you say. 'My name is Nimue.'

I touch the rose to my cheek. It is hot.

'And the brachet?' I say.

You laugh then. 'The brachet was nothing, Merlin, the merest excuse. I did not come for the brachet. I came for you.'

I bow with the rose in my hand. 'But why have you come for me? What should a young girl want with a dirty old man in a forest?'

You laugh again. 'Oh, people will say it was magic, to be sure. But I have no need of your magic, my Merlin. Nimue is mistress of all the craft, and Merlin is a man accomplishing his own ruin. You can tell me nothing I cannot guess.'

'I believe you,' I say. 'But take this story, for a start. Black book, white book, red book, gold . . . What does that mean to you, my young enchantress?'

'Alchemy.'

'Go on.'

'Black and white and red and gold are just the four stages of the alchemical process.'

'In which?'

'In which the contents of the alchemical retort is the unconscious of the alchemist.'

'Yes, yes. And then?'

'Well . . . Only fools suppose the alchemist looks for gold. I mean the metal. The most precious trash.' You lean back your head against the root of a great elm and stare up at the moon. 'Alchemy is metaphors,' you say. 'The alchemist works on himself. His *prima materia* is *him*. He labours to transmute the base matter of his dreams into gold.'

'And this poor alchemist?' I ask you.

'You, my dear? You started with gold, Merlin. You have turned it all into base matter, haven't you?'

There are tears in your hard eyes.

'But it is not too late yet,' you say, touching my hand. 'I have come to bring you back to the gold.'

19

'I'm not eggs-eggs-eggs-exactly an author-author-authority on Glass Castles,' admits Queen Guinevere. 'But it seems to me that this one has the shakes.'

'You drink too much,' says Sir Lancelot, at the mescal.

They are in the royal bedroom of the Grail Castle.

It is half past two in the morning.

The glass clock strikes.

The ground shakes once.

'There!' shrieks Queen Guinevere, shivering. 'Didn't you feel that?'

She is lying face-down on the bed and clutching the pillows as though frightened she'll fall off the world.

Sir Lancelot sucks at his drink and advances upon her.

'It's the forest,' he says. 'Some of these trees have long roots.'

'O Lance-Lance-Lancelot . . .'

At a quarter to three the castle shakes again and some glass splinters down from the roof.

'O Lance-Lance-Lancelot . . .'

The great queen's champion sits up in bed. He has the mescal in his one hand and his moustache in the other. An anxious leer improves his face.

'It's the hart and the hounds,' he says. 'They're running round and round in the hall down there. It's the vibrations.'

The mescal bottle is empty. He throws it away.

'Vibrations,' says Queen Guinevere, neglected.

King Arthur stands by the bedside, smiling, smiling. He has a look of unalterable boredom on his face which is blue and like one of the masks of God. His eyes show clearly bright and pale in contrast. He fondles the brachet and searches its coat for fleas.

'King,' says Sir Lancelot, wringing mescal from his moustache, 'be a good sport and pop down and tell Perceval to take his armour off and chase that white hart and those sixty black hounds right on out and into the forest of Broceliande, will you?'

'Good thinking,' says Queen Guggy. 'And when the lovely boy has done that send him straight back up here with his boots on!'

'I will,' says good King Arthur.

He is half-way out of the glass door of the royal bedroom when a thought occurs to him, and then he turns back to his friend and his queen on the bed and he says:

'But what about me? What can I do?'

'Perhaps we'll let you whah-whah-*watch*,' says Guinevere.

20

So this is brave Sir Perceval's big moment. It is better than the black sheep and the white sheep jumping backwards and forward across the river by the burning tree that was one side green. It is better than the black chessmen and the white chessmen that moved and won and lost of their own accord. It is better even than the black raven and the white snow and the black hair of his beloved that was blacker than the raven and the white skin of his beloved that was whiter than the snow.

Sir Perceval strips off his blue cap.

Sir Perceval strips off his blue cloak.

Sir Perceval strips off his blue breeches.

He roars a little bit of his favourite carol:

Cherries for me!

Then he starts to the chase.

Round the hall of the Grail Castle runs the white hart.

Round the hall of the Grail Castle run the sixty black hounds.

Round the hall of the Grail Castle runs Sir Perceval.
(He has kept his boots on, stained with summer dust.)
The glass clock strikes three times.
And the whole Grail Castle falls down.

21

'Don't tell me,' groans my uncle Beelzebub. 'Red worms and white worms?'

'Not at all,' my father says. 'Nothing so low and metaphysical. Just sex and mescal!'

My uncle the count Astarot hiccups.

'I never set up to be an engineer,' he mumbles. 'Especially not an engineer in glass. Glass is tricky stuff. Glass is nearly as tricky as women.'

My daddy the devil giggles.

'There's only one thing for it,' he announces. 'We'll have to get my son to build it for us.'

'His own tomb?' cry my uncles. 'He'll never do it!'

'Leave that to Nimue,' says the devil with a smile.

He spins on his ivory heels and points at Astarot:

'Now you get back inside Sir L, and pronto!'

He jerks his blasting rod at uncle B:

'And you get back to the once and future Cuckold!'

Beelzebub sighs.

'And how do we explain it all to Gug-Gug and to Perceval? The castle falling round their ears? *Unusual*, isn't it?'

'They are on a Quest,' says the Emperor Lucifer grandly. 'When you are on a Quest you have to expect the unusual, by definition. Besides, no damage has been done. The sixty black hounds have all run off, and the damned white hart's gone with them. We shan't be bothered by that sort of uroborus any more.'

He lies down on the floor of hell and writhes as another thought strikes him.

'Give Guinevere a shot of Perceval under the greenwood tree,' he says. 'By the time that's over they'll both have forgotten the fall of the Grail Castle. I've heard of humans likening what they call their orgasms to earthquakes. Romantic humans, that is. Our sort. And these creatures are romantics, have no doubt.'

But he adds, to be double certain:

'Make sure he keeps his boots on.'

22

Dawn comes like a green reluctant ghost to the forest of Broceliande.

Your white palfrey has stumbled and broken its forelock.

I put the poor animal out of its pain.

You mount before me on my black mare. Your hair is blown into my mouth.

Your hair tastes of sunlight.

You sing as we ride.

'Black,' you sing.

'White,' you sing.

'Red,' you sing.

'Gold,' you sing.

I do not like to ask you the song's meaning, or even where we may be going. It is enough for me that you ride with me. It is enough for me that you're in my arms. It is enough for me that you are singing. Sometimes you have my mother's voice, and sometimes Igrayne's, and sometimes Morgan's.

Once there is much yelping and barking and then the white hart runs towards us out of the trees and the sixty black hounds run after it and stream away past us, vanishing into the forest where we have ridden already.

You laugh.

I feel the small bones tremble in your shoulders as you laugh.

You take no notice otherwise of hart or hounds.

No birds sing.

The bright sun gives no heat.

But the green woods all around are a sun-filled Grail.

23

We come at last into a long green glade. There are oak trees on three sides, including the side through which we have ridden in entering it. The fourth side of the green glade is quite empty. It is an absence or a vacuum. There is nothing there. As though the blue sky has been turned inside-out and the other side of the sky has no colour at all.

The glade is filled with a lake which is the colour of steel made blue by fire.

On a stone in the heart of the lake I see a heron with a weasel in its beak.

'I have been here before,' I tell you.

'We have been here before,' you say. 'This is where we were before you were Merlin and I was Nimue. This is the *Val Sans Retour*. This is Diana's lake.'

By the side of the lake I see a marble tomb.

'In that tomb,' you tell me, 'Prince Faunus is buried.'

'Faunus,' I say. (I am trying to remember.)

'Faunus,' you say. 'Faunus, whom Diana loved much, but whom she killed by the greatest disloyalty of the world.'

'*In* the world?' I say.

'No. *Of* the world,' you tell me.

'Tell me,' I say. 'Tell me, tell me, tell me, Nimue.'

'Tell me how Diana killed her Faunus,' I beg you.

You tell me.

'Diana,' you say, 'as you well know, Merlin, reigned at the time of Virgil, long before the birth of Christ. She loved these woods above all. After having hunted in all the woods of France and of Brittany, she came here, she settled by the side of this lake, and had built here her manor by great enchantment. She lived for a long time in this wood. And the son of the king to whom all this country then belonged fell in love with her, left his home and his parents and lived with her here in her manor. His name was Prince Faunus.'

'Diana's manor,' I say.

'Soon after,' you say, 'Diana met another knight, whilst she was hunting. His name was Felix. She became enamoured of him. Felix, though a brave knight, was poor. He feared the power of Prince Faunus. Therefore he did not dare venture to return Diana's passion. To overcome this obstacle, Diana resolved to murder Faunus.'

'Prince Faunus must die,' I say.

(Is it my voice that says it?)

'Near the lake,' you go on, 'was a tomb that was filled with enchanted waters, having the power to heal all sorts of wounds. One day Faunus, sorely wounded by a wild beast, repaired to the healing waters, but found them gone. Diana had drained them away in the night. Now Diana advised him to enter the grave undressed, saying that she would cover it and put in wholesome herbs, which would soon heal him.'

'Naked into the tomb,' I say.

'Faunus,' you say, 'suspecting nothing wrong, did as Diana told him. When the lid was put on the tomb, Diana had melted lead poured into it, so that Faunus died a terrible death. Then Diana went to Felix and told him how she had rid herself of Faunus. The story of her unnatural cruelty so disgusted Felix that he drew his sword, seized hold of Diana's hair, and with one stroke cut her head from her body.'

'Cruel Felix,' I say.

'The body of Diana,' you go on, 'was thrown into this lake you see before you. And for this reason it has ever afterwards been called Diana's lake.'

'And what became of Diana's manor?' I ask you.

'The father of Prince Faunus destroyed it,' you tell me, 'and everything else that belonged to Diana, after his son's murder.'

On a stone in the heart of the lake: a heron with a weasel in its beak.

24

'Herons do not catch weasels,' says my uncle Beelzebub.

'No,' says the devil my father. 'But they do catch Antichrists.'

Astarot is jumping up and down and gnawing his tail.

'This Perceval's going too far!' he shouts. 'And to hell with romanticism!'

'Rule two of demonic possession,' observes my dad. 'Do not get identified with the possessed to your own unbalance.'

'But some of these knights would do incubi out of a job .. Just look at him, Shiner!'

The Emperor Lucifer considers Sir Perceval's boots where they drum between Guinevere's legs.

'OK,' he says. 'Have Lancelot sort him out!'

25

Sir Lancelot du Lac, moustaches abristle like the antennae of some most particular insect, creeps up behind the greenwood tree where Sir Perceval of Wales lies full-length and naked (save for his summer-speckled boots) on the body of Queen Gug-gug-gug-gug-Guinevere. Sir Lancelot fetches his rival knight a sharpish blow on the back of the head with his mace. At the same time he stamps very hard with his mailed foot on Perceval's bum.

'Aaaarrrgh!' observes Sir Perceval.

'Th-th-th-th-*thank* you!' says Queen Guinevere.

26

'Merlin,' you say. 'I love Diana's lake.'

'Yes,' I say.

'I love the woods about the lake,' you say. 'I love the light between the trees. I love the colour of the lake.'

'Yes,' I say.
'It is like steel made blue by fire,' you say. 'The colour of the lake.'
'It is,' I say.
'I would like to live here for ever,' you say.
I say nothing.
'I would like to pass my life here,' you say.
I say nothing.
I toss a stone into the water.
'If you really loved me, Merlin . . .'
'Yes,' I say.
'If you really loved me, Merlin, I think that you would make again Diana's manor, and live beside me here.'
'Diana's manor?'
'The Grail Castle.'
I look into your eyes and see myself.
'Could you make me such a manor, Merlin? Could you?'
'Yes,' I say.
'And would you?'
'Yes,' I say.
You take my hands in your hands.
'And will you, Merlin? Will you? Will you?'
'If that is what you really want,' I say.
You answer me nothing. There is a green leaf in your hair.
At last you say:
'Merlin, I lied to you about the death of Diana. She lies *with* Faunus in the tomb. They are like king and queen, Sol and Luna, in the alchemical work, shrouded in each other's arms for ever. Do you understand me?'
'Yes,' I say.
I understand you better than you know.
Then you say:
'I cannot live with you in your Grail Castle, Merlin. But I will give you friends to keep you company. A little wolf. An apple tree. A pig called Jesus.'
I laugh. I kiss you on your mouth.
'I am your gold,' you say.
'And I am your base matter,' I reply.

27

End. Again. End again, little pig. End with the *Morte Darthur* and the Sleeve Job.

I made Diana's manor for you, Nimue.

It fills the fourth side of the forest glade.

It is the Grail Castle. It is Merlin's tomb. It is the esplumoir, the cage of the moulting hawk, the place of transformation. It is the house whose walls are winds. It is my crystal cave. It is a wilderness of hawthorn. It is the tree that is one side flames and the other side green leaves growing.

And even as I made it I heard my own voice saying: *Whom does the Grail serve?*

And I saw again the sword thrust into the stone, and the lance thrust bleeding into the golden cup.

I know you now, Merlin Ambrosius.

You are your devils, Merlin Silvester.

As for the other people in my story . . .

Queen Guinevere went and hied herself to a nunnery. But it was the black-walled convent of the Flaming Heart, where Morgan le Fay was now the abbess. So I hardly like to think about their penance.

Sir Lancelot went mad and turned into a werewolf, to the delight of the Fair Maid of Astarot.

As for King Arthur and his bastard Mordred: I was privileged to see the last of them from my Glass Castle.

Mordred in black armour rode to kill the king. King Arthur ran at Mordred with his spear so that the spear went right through Mordred's body and out the other side.

'Father! My father!' Mordred cries. He thrusts himself forward along the spear that is killing him. He drags himself on. He crawls slowly, hanging by his wound. He hauls himself inch by inch to reach the king.

Tears pour down King Arthur's face to see his son struggling to touch him in his death agony. He snatches off his helmet. He holds his arms out for a last embrace. He bends to kiss Mordred's cheek.

And Mordred's knife goes into his father's mouth and cuts and cuts. He cuts away Arthur's face.

Mordred falls dead at his father's feet.

King Arthur falls over him, blinded, his eyes cut out.

King Arthur is wounded, mortally.

A knight called Sir Bedivere unclasps the sword Excalibur from Arthur's hand. He winds the gold-embroidered leather scabbard about the hilt. He stands upon the bank of the lake which is like steel made blue by fire, Diana's lake. He braces himself for a mighty throw.

Out, out, flashing far in the moonlight, the sword Excalibur.

It falls in a shining arc down into the dark waters.

And there a hand catches it, and holds it, and shakes it three times.

An arm swathed in samite, that vanishes into the lake.

(It is Nimue's hand, of course, O my Jesukin.)

Now here are three queens in mourning in a black barge on the water.

They bear away Arthur no man knows where.

(Unwise the thought: a grave for Arthur.)

The first queen has the face of the virgin Vivien.

The second queen has the face of the Lady Igrayne.

The third queen has the face of the King's half-sister, Queen Morgan le Fay.

Now, without sail, without oars, the draped barge passes out from the shore.

It is black upon the waters, and then gold.

Little pig, listen.

The wind in the reeds.

The laughter of Merlin!

28

'And the next morning,' says the devil my father, 'Sir Perceval woke in the great hall of the Grail Castle and he found his blue cap and his blue cloak and his blue breeches lying in a heap beside him, and his sword and his armour also, but no one answered his call and came to help him to arm. And Sir Perceval put on his blue cap and his blue cloak and his blue breeches, and buckled on his sword and his armour unaided. And he walked from the great hall of the Grail Castle, finding all its glass doors locked save the door on the moving wheel by which he had entered. And there was no one to answer Sir Perceval's knocking and calling. And in the courtyard Sir Perceval found his horse waiting, saddled, and bridled, and the gate was open and the moving wheel was still. And Sir Perceval rode forth from the Grail Castle. And while he was on the moving wheel it began to spin, so that he had to spur his horse forward to jump to reach the world again. And then Sir Perceval turned, and he cried out a great challenge. *Merlin!* he shouted. *Merlin! Merlin! Merlin!* But the castle was silent and answer came there none, and nothing remained for Sir Perceval but to be on his way. And when he reached the end of the lake and rode into the forest again, Sir Perceval looked back for a last time. And the Grail Castle was gone. The Grail Castle was as if it had never been.'

Lucifer laughs like a clock running down.

Then he blows an imperfect smoke ring perfectly.

29

'And Sir Perceval grinned,' say my uncle Astarot and my uncle Beelzebub together, 'Sir Perceval grinned like a fox eating shit out of a wire brush.'

30

'Now there's this knight still up a tree in the forest of Broceliande,' says my uncle Astarot. 'His name is Sir Gawain. He's young. He's tall. He's handsome. He's romantic. He's dressed in a surcoat of rich red satin and a mantle all of crimson, trimmed with gold. On his head there's a cap of purple velvet. His feet and his legs are clad in fine leather. Gold bosses on his shoes. Well, he's been missing all the fun, and he got cramp and pins and needles sitting up with the squirrels and the owls all night, but now at last he is riding along through the forest singing *Tirra lirra* and looking for Quests and adventures and he meets this young damsel weeping by a fountain, see? A very classy piece. Educated. Cultured. She speaks in blank verse, as a matter of fact. A real queen. A perfect princess. Plays the dulcimer probably. If you laid a ruler against her two feet, it would be hard to find any fault with either of them. Now, Sir Gawain is looking for the Holy Grail, like everyone else. So naturally he refrains from dragging her off into the bushes and fucking all hell out of her. The damsel is deeply impressed. This is the first knight of the Round Table who ever met her weeping by this particular fountain who didn't have her up against a tree and her French knickers down in fifteen minutes. (They're sheerest samite, if you want to know, with an interesting gusset.) So the damsel says, by way of reward for his respect for her: "Good knight, what is your name?" "Gawain of Verulam," says Sir Gawain. "Well then, Gawain," the damsel tells him, "I will do for you what I have never done for any knight before. *Have you heard of the Sleeve Job?"* Gawain is tempted. In fact he falls off his horse. The damsel takes his hand and leads him into the darkest part of the forest. But when they reach it, Gawain loses his nerve. He kneels before the damsel, and begs her to forgive him. He urges her also to leave this terrible life of weeping and soliciting in King Arthur's forests. "Will you marry me?" he says. She's a lovely lovely creature, in great need of reformation, so she says she will, assuring him through her tears of gratitude that she will give him the promised and forbidden Sleeve Job on their wedding night. "After all," she says, "it won't be so bad if we're man and wife." Then Sir Gawain rides with the damsel into Camelot. He introduces her to the other knights, and she is presented at court to King Arthur and Queen Guinevere. (This is before Arthur got Mordred and Guggy got the abbess of the Flaming Heart.) Everybody fancies her. Everybody thinks that Sir Gawain has made an outstanding choice. At last, after seven long years of betrothal, during which Gawain has worn none but the damsel's favour and been faithful to her, utterly, the couple are married in Saint Paul's church by the archbishop of Canterbury. The bells ring. The choirs sing. The bride is stripped bare by her bachelors, even. Everyone withdraws, leaving Sir Gawain and the damsel alone in the bedroom together. "Now," says our good knight, "now what about it?" "What about what?" says the damsel. "Your promise," says Gawain of Verulam. "I shall keep it," says the damsel, adding: "I'll obey you, I'll serve you, I'll love and honour and keep you in sickness and in health, and forsaking all other – " "Never mind that," says Gawain. "*What about the Sleeve Job?*" he reminds her. The damsel screams. She had forgotten. She runs to the window, naked as she is, and threatens to jump out. "Fuck me!" she cries. "Beg pardon?" says Gawain. "Fuck me! Bugger me! Anything you like!" the damsel cries. "But *not the Sleeve Job*! Please! Please! I must have been mad ever to suggest it . . . Anything but that!" Of course, all this makes Sir Gawain only the keener. He's obsessed with it now. *He must have the Sleeve Job*. Nothing else will do. He rubs her breasts against his chest. She tempts him with her bum. "No!" says Gawain firmly. "*I want the Sleeve Job!*" At last, in tears, the damsel relents. "O very well," she sobs. "Since I promised you . . . And you *are* my husband . . ." Gawain is now beside himself! He kisses the tears from her eyes! *The Sleeve Job!* His rod sticks up straight against his belly at the thought of it! The damsel smiles and blushes. A hard little light of excitement begins in her eyes too, as she fingers him, and feels him press against her tender flesh. "Go into the bathroom," she whispers. "The bathroom?" says Gawain of Verulam. "The bathroom," says the damsel. "Go into the bathroom and lather yourself. I want you stark naked and covered from top to toe with soap. Every little part, my darling. And every big part too! Thoroughly thoroughly soaped. Then come back to me here, and *you shall have the Sleeve Job . . .*"

"O my love," cries Sir Gawain. And Sir Gawain does just as the young enchantress has told him. He goes into the bathroom and heats water. He lathers himself from top to bottom. He is covered in, smothered in soap. Singing! *Tirra lirra!* Dripping with soap-suds! His member is sticking up huge and dripping too! He leaps from the bathtub! *Tirra lirra!* He is on his way! Sir Gawain! He is running to his love! Naked! Soapy! All ready! *The Sleeve Job!* THE SLEEVE JOB! *Now!* But what's this? Running, Sir Gawain's right foot alights on a little tiny insignificant cake of soap . . . He slips! He skids! *Sir Gawain!* Sliding! Falling! Sir GAW – AIN! All knightly shining soapy six feet six inches of him falling falling falling . . .'

'And?' says my father the devil.

'What happens next?' says my uncle the prince Beelzebub.

'Nothing happens next,' says Astarot.

'Nothing?' says Beelzebub.

'Nothing happens next,' says Astarot. 'There ain't no next. *This is the end.*'

'But Sir Gawain?' says my father.

'Brained himself on the iron bed,' says my uncle Astarot.

'But the Sleeve Job?' says my uncle Beelzebub.

'Ah yes, the Sleeve Job,' says my uncle Astarot. 'Well, Sir Gawain being dead and gone, he never did find out what the Sleeve Job is.'

'So how can this be the end of it all?' screams my father.

My uncle the count Astarot holds up his right hand in blessing.

'I didn't say it was the end of it all,' he says, choosing his words with care. 'There was and is and shall be no end of it all. Ever. World without end, remember?' He grins from ear to ear and crosses himself with his tail. 'Begin,' he says. 'Again,' he says. 'Begin again,' he says. *'This is just the end of the story,'* he explains.

1-800-228-3311